EMPOWER YOUR PRESENCE

How to Build True Wealth
with Your Personal Brand and Image

CATHERINE BELL

KNOWLEDGE BUREAU
NEWSBOOKS

WINNIPEG, MANITOBA, CANADA

Catherine Bell

EMPOWER YOUR PRESENCE
How to Build True Wealth with Your Personal Brand and Image

Printed and bound in Canada

Library and Archives Canada Cataloguing in Publication

Bell, Catherine Graham, 1951-, author
Empower your presence : how to build true wealth
with your personal brand and image / Catherine Bell.

Includes index.
ISBN 978-1-927495-16-2 (pbk.)

    1. Self-perception. 2. Self-presentation. 3. Interpersonal communication. 4. Clothing and dress. 5. Success. 6. Success in business. I. Title.

BF697.5.S43B44 2013   158.1   C2013-906614-4

Published by:
Knowledge Bureau, Inc.
187 St. Mary's Road, Winnipeg, Manitoba Canada R2H 1J2
204-953-4769
Email: reception@knowledgebureau.com

Publisher: Evelyn Jacks
Editor: Nicole Chartrand
Cover Design and Layout: Evelyn Jacks and Carly Thompson
Page Design and layout: Karen Armstrong Graphic Design

Table of Contents

Foreward

What does it take to walk into a room with presence? We all know people who can do that with ease. They have the wow factor! Everyone wants to talk to them. They are articulate, warm, friendly, and funny; they can eat the hors d'oeuvres and carry on with conversations that attract a crowd, without spilling a drop! Even if they do, it seems, well, cool!

What's so special about them? How have they developed that powerful charisma and style that is both jaw-dropping and deserving of respect?

To begin, they project great confidence in their own abilities, because they understand their personal vision and goals. They can connect with others well, because they are not afraid to become engaged and share emotions and their dreams for the future. They are poised to do well financially too, because they have the traits of great leaders.

These are the influencers: people with an empowered presence who understand what impact they have on others. They can draw people to them, not only because of what they do or say or how they dress, but mostly because of *who and what they are:* consistently genuine with an external style that compliments their internal strengths.

They are truly wealthy, from the inside out; they know that an influential, empowered presence is never about the money… *it's about relationships*.

If you are interested in building this kind of empowered presence for yourself – a memorable one because it flows from within – you need to read this book. Catherine Bell has done something very special for you: she brings to you her engaging experience and authority in sharing essential tips for building true wealth, with your personal brand and image.

Catherine Bell, in fact, is that kind of person. She is compelling and engaging; I can vouch for that because I first met her in an elevator. Her personal appearance and style was striking, she exuded a friendly confidence in her bright smile, and as she sold herself to me in a classic "elevator pitch" that ended perfectly when the elevator doors opened, I was wowed! She's a natural.

But make no mistake, an empowered presence is multi-faceted; it requires planning, and it is earned over time. In fact, it's a result of a deliberate self investment. As Catherine will share with you, that's especially important these days because the image you project is potentially everywhere... not just in elevators.

It's embodied in your email communications, social media and personal interactions. Your empowered personal presence will compel others to follow you, to "like" your comments in social media, drive miles to meet with you, hire you, publish your book or otherwise invest in you - all because you are just that awesome.

I am certain that with Catherine by your side, you too can empower your presence and exude charisma and confidence – the kind that will result in a reputation well-earned and sought after by family and strangers alike.

Catherine takes you on a journey in which you will learn to confidently define and present yourself, so you can enhance your ability to get a job, lead a team, coach a winning organization, or even engage in lifelong relationships. You'll learn how to consistently demonstrate characteristics that will draw people to you and want to work and be with you. But more than that, she will challenge you to dig deeper and understand what true wealth – what I like to define as a deep satisfaction and peace of mind – means to you, so you can share it with others.

That's what this book is about, and I am so glad Catherine and I met in that elevator, because we are so proud at Knowledge Bureau, to have published this, her second book, just for you.

Evelyn Jacks, President
Knowledge Bureau Newsbooks

Acknowledgements

I wish to acknowledge several people who assisted and inspired me during the writing of this book. My thanks go to Evelyn Jacks of Knowledge Bureau for encouraging me to utilize my expertise to address a topic that is dear to my heart – something that I'm sure will encourage people to be confident and strong. I appreciated the time that friend and colleague, Deborah King of Final Touch Finishing School took to review my material on dining etiquette, to ensure that I presented a balanced view in areas that image consultants around the world continue to discuss and debate. I'm grateful for Diane Black's illustrations that clearly help to demonstrate proper behaviour at the table. My thanks go to body language experts Patti Wood and Mark Bowden, who have given me a deeper understanding of how powerful our non verbal communication is and how we can use it to influence people's responses to us. I appreciate Dr. P. M. Forni's world-renowned work on civility; Dan Stelter's insights on the strengths of shy people; Carrie Ballone, Adwoa Buahene and Giselle Kovary's writings on multi-generational perspectives in the workplace; and Roy Williams and Vic Preisser's research on the transition of family wealth to the next generation. I want to mention all the valuable insights I've received over the years from my clients, students, friends, family and colleagues, especially members of the Association of Image Consultants International who free share their expertise involving appearance, behaviour and communication. Thanks to everyone who contributed their insights on what true wealth means to them. My editor, Nicole Chartrand, was always delightful to work with and her sense of humour, skills and insights were instrumental in further refining my writing. Most importantly, my love and thanks go to my husband, Gregory, who had the patience to read and re-read the evolving text of this book. His awareness of history and contemporary culture, and his uncanny ability to suggest just the right word when I was at a loss, added so much to the process. His unwavering support and positive reinforcement of everything I do assists me in continually empowering my presence.

The Magnitude of Presence

I once had the privilege of hosting a table at an afternoon tea held to honour Her Royal Highness Princess Anne – the Princess Royal. She was to be the guest speaker later that evening at March of Dimes Canada's annual Ability and Beyond Gala held to raise funds for programs that assist people with physical disabilities to live independently. The hosts had all been duly prepared with protocol on how to greet the Princess and introduce her to the others at their tables, telling her a little about each person and their connection with the organization.

All eyes were on Princess Anne as she entered the room and began moving systematically from table to table, ours being the last of ten for her to visit. Security guards swarmed around her, some walking into the adjacent room near us to ensure that when the tea was over, it would be safe to take that route to the next carefully orchestrated event. Things were behind schedule when Princess Anne reached us, and my mind was going through the names of the people I was about to introduce. Without thinking, I reached out and grasped her hand with my usual business-like firmness. I immediately felt her gloved fingers drawing back from mine. I was horrified. I'd forgotten to shake her hand lightly and of course could think of nothing else as we sat down.

Princess Anne gracefully overlooked my faux pas and immediately began conversing with the people on either side of her, asking about March of Dimes and its origins in the 50s when mothers marched from door to door collecting dimes so that a cure for poliomyelitis could be found. A few minutes later, she suddenly swung around to face me and asked, "And when did you have polio?" Given that she had just met over a hundred people, not only was I impressed with her ability to remember this detail from my brief introduction, but it was her manner. Her gaze was totally fixed upon me and she listened attentively for my reply. Even with her tight itinerary, it was as if she had all the time in the world. I'll never forget her ability to be completely present in that moment, as if no one else was in the room with us.

We all know people who, although they are not of royal personage, immediately capture our attention in the same way. What compels us to take notice? I'm not referring to people whose physique or loud voice is overpowering and intimidating, keeping us at a distance, but those who have that distinct magnetism that draws us closer. There's something about them that is intriguing and difficult to articulate, but we know that they possess the power to captivate.

What is it about their enthralling presence that makes you want to spend time with them? Sometimes it is hard to identify why you hang on the person's every word. Does she make you feel good, even though you don't have everything together? Does he encourage you to be confident when facing new challenges? Is it that the person is totally focused on you when you are speaking, as I experienced with Princess Anne? I'm sure there are many reasons that people have a certain charisma and poise that is so attractive. We want to shadow them to learn from their actions and be inspired. Sometimes, even just a few minutes with them can be so transformational.

What is Presence?

Presence has a multitude of meanings, from simply being physically close to someone, to an awareness of an unseen spiritual entity. People with a domineering presence frequently use fear to control and manipulate people. This type of presence usually requires continual vigilance to maintain the power that it wields, and as such does not last. Other people have a certain effortless poise and charm that is all encompassing.

I believe that presence is not about being overbearing, but about being completely available to the people or situations in which you find yourself. It is about engagement and personal connection with one person – or 1000 people. It is about how you carry yourself, being poised and comfortable in your own skin. It involves a certain charismatic attraction with people that happens naturally, and it is not just for the privileged few – we can all have presence.

The Oxford Dictionary defines presence as: *"the state or fact of existing, occurring, or being present; the impressive manner or appearance of a person."*[1] Other sources define it as *"a person's bearing, especially when it commands respectful attention,"*[2] and a *"dignified personality."*[3] Even the definition associated with stage presence, *"the quality of self-assurance and effectiveness that permits a performer to achieve a rapport with the audience,"*[4] can be applied to our encounter with those we meet on a daily basis, who are in a sense, our audience.

Physical attractiveness can increase one's presence, but relying totally on one's looks isn't sustainable. The source of true presence must be deep inside you. I'm sure that you can think of many people who have presence whose outward characteristics alone would not command attention, and yet they have an ability to draw you in with seemingly little effort on their part – perhaps it is because of the way they treat others, the wisdom they share, or maybe the way they speak. There is always something about them that transcends our visual impression.

How does Presence Lead to True Wealth?

The magnitude of presence is that it can create meaningful relationships and change lives in deep ways, and in doing so, build true wealth for everyone involved. It is not something that you use to achieve great things solely for yourself, but a source of motivational good that can positively influence and empower others.

How does this happen? You don't need to be mature in years or rich in terms of possessions to have presence, nor do you fly in to save people from themselves and manipulate outcomes.

---

[1] http://oxforddictionaries.com/definition/english/presence?q=presence

[2] The American Heritage® Dictionary of the English Language, Fourth Edition copyright 2000 by Houghton Mifflin Company. Updated in 2009.

[3] Collins English Dictionary – Complete and Unabridged © HarperCollins Publishers 1991, 1994, 1998, 2000, 2003

[4] The American Heritage® Dictionary of the English Language, Fourth Edition copyright 2000 by Houghton Mifflin Company. Updated in 2009.

Instead, push your agenda completely out of the way and make yourself totally available to others so that you will be able to recognize their intrinsic attributes. When you affirm and encourage people to embrace and use these, meaningful relationships develop. These relationships are at the core of true wealth.

Shyness and Presence

People with presence are not always outwardly strong and confident. This is true with people who are shy. Typically, when shy people compare themselves to those who are outgoing, they are hard on themselves because they feel that they do not measure up. They are not aware of the positive impact they can have on others.

When Dan Stelter, author of the *Anxiety Support Network*[5], was a guest writer on the *Life Optimizer* blog,[6] he listed these seven things that shy people often see as weaknesses, which actually are positive traits and I believe they add to an empowered presence:

1. **Cautious thinking:** When faced with difficult problems, carefully thinking through things instead of making snap decisions will result in positive outcomes. This can add to one's reputation, increasing personal and professional success.

2. **Meekness can make you approachable:** People are more comfortable approaching someone who is not aggressive and outspoken, potentially setting the stage for establishing beneficial relationships.

3. **Being quiet leads to a calming effect on others:** People view someone who is quiet as being calm, which can have a profound, positive impact during times of crises and turmoil.

4. **Appearing vulnerable is great for certain jobs:** In various human-service sectors, such as counselling or therapy, appearing vulnerable as many shy people do, encourages others to feel safe and open up.

5. **Shy people appear to be innocent or good:** Compared to forceful individuals, people respect and trust those who are less dominant, opening

---

5   http://www.anxietysupportnetwork.com/index.php
6   Stelter, Dan, "7 Strengths Shy People Have," 2012, http://www.lifeoptimizer. org/2011/04/08/strengths-shy-people-have/

up many possibilities for them to connect with others and broaden their networks.

6. **Shy people tend to be more believable:** Aggressive, outgoing people sometimes are viewed as self-serving; whereas, shy people give the impression that their interests are not central so they are believed and trusted.

7. **Being shy leads individuals to learn how to overcome barriers:** Shy people who want to be successful know that their shyness could hold them back from involvement in things most others enjoy with ease. When it is important, they will usually find a way around obstacles and continually look for opportunities to improve.

From an early age, Mahatma Gandhi was a very shy person. In fact, even as a lawyer in his early 30s, he could barely speak in front of a judge. He was unsuccessful in his profession, until he found the right cause and set about overcoming stumbling blocks created by his shyness. I am sure most people would agree that Gandhi, one of the major political and spiritual leaders of his time, had great presence and profoundly influenced the world.

What Does Presence Mean to You?

Presence is very personal. What impresses one person is not of value to another, so the first step in empowering your presence is to identify what it means to you. The following questions will assist you with this discovery and the creation of your fundamental master list of the characteristics that you associate with an empowered presence. These are likely the characteristics you would want to see in yourself. Throughout the book, refer back to this master list as we look at true wealth and personal branding and go on to carefully align the ABCs of your image – appearance, behaviour and communication – to ensure that the message you want to convey to others consistently reflects who you really are.

Who comes to mind when you think about people with presence? Celebrities may immediately surface; however, there are many others who have touched you, usually at a more personal level, such as a relative, teacher, colleague, client, friend, etc. They may have had a profound influence either on you or on others you know, or perhaps have an intriguing charisma that you admire.

What are the reasons you've included these people on the list? Have they inspired you to continue your education? Are they kind? Do they make you feel good about yourself? Do they have a large group of friends? Are they experts in their fields? Are they strong, confident people, even when facing new challenges? Have they been successful in their careers? Have they an ability to remain calm in stressful situations? Are they wealthy? Are they spiritual? Have they had a global impact? Do people listen when they speak? There are no right or wrong reasons because your approach will be unique, but what you'll discover will help you identify what is important to you and what could help you achieve more presence.

What strengths, actions, skills, values, personal attributes, passions, etc. have these people used to inspire you? For example, if they make you feel good about yourself, is it because they encourage you when things are difficult, or on the other hand, do they challenge you to go beyond your comfort zone? Record as many observations as you can.

Usually you will find that a pattern emerges. Compile a master list of the most common characteristics that you admire in people with presence. For each item on your master list, think about how you would be empowered in your own life if you had this characteristic. For example, if one of the master list items was the ability to give polished presentations, what difference would this make to you? What would you be able to do? How could this improve your image, increase your presence and build true wealth?

Can Presence Be Learned?

Presence is something that can be cultivated and developed. Once you have identified the traits that you admire, the next step in empowering your presence is having a clear understanding of who you are and the value you bring to others. The personal branding process in Chapter 3 will assist you with this. Often people go through life with no thought of their passions, what is important to them, which skills and attributes guide the actions they are most proud of, and how these can be used to build deep relationships. Your presence will increase when you know exactly what you bring to the table and are equipped to deliver.

Many motivational speakers say that if you spend your life going from job to job, crisis to crisis, or relationship to relationship without ever changing what you do, the results will always be the same. If this sounds familiar, *Empower Your Presence* will encourage you to break this pattern by taking time to examine what is important to you. Expect to see positive results as you work your way through each chapter.

Living with an empowered presence is not about learning a few quick tips to make you stand out, but it involves aligning your intentions and everything in your environment with who you are, and then clearly communicating it to everyone you meet in an authentic and confident manner through your personal brand and image. You will find that the resulting relationships and confidence that develop will be a source of true wealth for you. We will now go on to examine what true wealth is and how you can move closer to having a magnitude of presence.

Chapter 1 - At A Glance

Charismatic Attraction

Having an empowered presence involves a charismatic attraction that captivates and holds attention. It is something that can be developed and cultivated by everyone.

Personal Connection and Engagement

The magnitude of presence is its ability to build meaningful relationships, deeply change people's lives, and in so doing, build true wealth for everyone involved.

Generous Empowerment and Affirmation

People with presence are generous, pushing their agendas aside, so that they can be completely present, recognize others' intrinsic values and empower them by reflecting back what they see in an affirming manner.

True Wealth Trumps Money

When most people hear the word "wealth," riches, affluence, and copious amounts of money come to mind. Wealth may conjure up images of being able to buy anything. It could involve world travel, staying in five-star hotels, and enjoying wonderful meals at each exotic location. Perhaps it has to do with being publically honoured for generous charitable gifts. Wealth does allow you the luxury of being financially secure, and the opportunity to be involved in activities beyond those necessary for daily sustenance; however there is so much more. Coco Chanel once said, "There are people who have money and people who are rich."

As soon as the word "*true*" is coupled with wealth, the meaning of the word is profoundly changed. True wealth extends far beyond mere currency to impacting lives in incredible ways, turning affluence into influence, which is at the centre of presence. I recognize that money is essential in our economy, and once our basic needs are met, it can be a vehicle for positive change. However, if all you have are monetary assets and your sole priority is to obtain more of the same, you'll always fall short of having true wealth. Let's examine what people associate with true wealth and how it plays a role in increasing your presence.

What is True Wealth?

If you were asked, "What is true wealth?" you'd expect your answer to be unique because it would be closely linked to your personal values. Surprisingly, when I posed this question to several people, immediately everyone said that it had nothing to do with money. Although each answer varied, three overall themes emerged. True wealth was associated with:

- Developing meaningful relationships
- Being fully engaged with life
- Having peace of mind

Developing Meaningful Relationships

CASE STUDY: Lauren[1], a mid-level executive, connected true wealth with the relationships she developed during her career, enabling her to move up the corporate ladder, and more importantly, have autonomy to manage a large team. She was presented with an opportunity for a promotion that required a letter of recommendation from her supervisor, a micro-manager, who closely monitoring everything Lauren did. In spite of the fact that under Lauren's guidance the department continually exceeded their annual targets, her manager always made her feel that her work fell short of expectations. Knowing this could negatively affect her promotion, Lauren approached colleagues with whom she had established good relationships over time, and asked them to write additional reference letters on her behalf. They readily agreed and Lauren obtained the promotion.

There is great value associated with the ability to develop meaningful relationships and the empowered presence that comes from knowing you are looked up to and can be counted on.

I'm sure that you know people who meet others easily and quickly connect at deep, rather than superficial levels. They get along with their family, have a variety of friends, and possibly have a life partner with whom to share their joys and sorrows. When they enter a room of strangers, they seem to move effortlessly from person to person. During work, at school or in the community, they inspire numerous people and can call on them at a moment's notice, as Lauren did.

Although you may think that these are idyllic examples, there are many people who fit these descriptions. Granted, some relationships will be deeper than others, but the key point is that the genuine connections you develop

---

[1] People mentioned in case studies are fictitious.

with people are more valuable than money, because your impact is far more reaching, adding to your true wealth, as well as that of others.

Some relationships form because of a natural chemistry you have with someone that gives immediate rapport. In other situations, you may think that an amount of personal change is required for relationships to develop or improve. Of course, this can be on either side. Be careful - expecting more of people than they are able to give can be damaging because no one likes the message that they must change in order to be accepted. It is important to respect the authenticity of each person. Perhaps, you may discover a mutual acquaintance that can assist, or eventually you might realize that change really isn't necessary to allow for collaboration.

It is possible for you to learn how to enhance your current relationships and build new ones, and in doing so, increase your influence and presence. One of the most important factors is giving to others – not money, but your time, support and attention. It is interesting to observe that when charismatic people rise in the ranks, frequently they become kinder and more generous.

The phrase "givers gain," which is often used in networking, has never been truer here. Giving away your time to genuinely listen to someone forms trust and ultimately enriches relationships. Communication plays such a huge role in this process. When in conversation, if you are self-centred, distracted, or immediately rush off as soon as a person finishes speaking, you will be discounted. If people realize that you truly care and are interested in them, they will rely on you, want to learn from you, and will go out of their way to assist when needed.

Being Fully Engaged with Life

CASE STUDY: Patrick described true wealth as the exhilaration he felt when he graduated from college, not because of the money he hoped to earn, but because he was the first member in his immediate family to do so. This is something that people who come from families where post-secondary education is a tradition often take for granted. Many institutions encourage first generation college students with special incentives, recognizing the significant step they have taken to enroll and how difficult it is for them to complete their programs. Patrick's success opened up many career options for him personally, as well as other opportunities to make a positive impact in his community. In addition to finding employment in his field, he volunteers with an organization that encourages teens to graduate from high school.

Being fully engaged with life covers so many areas. For Patrick, it involved the courage to overcome the mindset and stigma associated with never being good enough to obtain a college diploma. Education is empowering because the knowledge and skills gained through it can fuel your curiosity and creativity, increasing your character and confidence. Through Patrick's persistence and the use of positive self-talk, which can affect outcomes, his doubt was transformed into a drive to move forward. Instead of accepting the status quo, he became an agent of change. His work with at-risk youth continues to build his presence and true wealth as he helps them visualize the success that is possible.

Being happy at work also plays a central role in engagement. When there is continuous learning and growth, and collaborative leaders who involve staff in significant projects, people look forward to going to work. Even if you are completely fatigued at the end of the day, there is great joy that comes from employment where you can use your vision, mind, and talents, especially when you are achieving goals and having a positive impact. In my career, I've always experienced this; however, I realize that this is not the case for everyone.

A survey on employee satisfaction[2] done in the US and Canada by Right Management, a subsidiary of a large staffing firm, ManpowerGroup, concluded that the majority of people were not satisfied with their jobs. When the economy is lacklustre, it is difficult for people to improve their situation by moving to other employment. One thing that was found to increase staff engagement when pay raises were not possible was involving employees directly in delivering good customer service. This opportunity to create good relationships provided a deep satisfaction that was equated with wealth in their minds. When people have the power to make a difference with customers, their self-worth and loyalty are also increased.

I'm not ignoring the fact that work isn't always equated with true wealth, but that employment also provides the means to enable people to pursue

---

[2] "Majority of Employees Don't Find Job Satisfying," May 2012, http://www.right.com/news-and-events/press-releases/2012-press-releases/item23352.aspx

fulfilling activities in their private time. I find this especially true with younger people who have a global sense of social responsibility. Unlike many workaholic Baby Boomers who have a keen focus on their careers, people born in the mid sixties and later are not content with just having a job. They also want to make a difference in the world, through volunteering during their holidays with a cause they support, starting charities, raising funds using social media and other innovative means, etc. Retired people who are in good health are also staying fully engaged in life by volunteering. Whether they are assisting with disaster relief, digging wells to provide clean water, helping people to improve their literacy skills, or a plethora of other humanitarian and creative endeavours, their contributions make a difference that goes beyond words. There is more to say about specific generational characteristics that influence presence and true wealth in a later chapter.

Having Peace of Mind

CASE STUDY: When I asked Rosario about true wealth, she said that it was not about having a large bank account, but being able to provide for her family with just one job so that her children would never feel anxious. She was the oldest of four children, and her mother was a single parent who continually had to work two or three jobs to make ends meet. Even though the family was together and the children were loved, her mother's anxiety obviously influenced their peace of mind. Rosarlo's relationships with her children are precious and she will do everything that she can to make sure that financial uncertainty and anxiety will not rob them of having piece of mind.

Peace of mind can have such a variety of meanings. It has to do with the harmony created when many things in your life come together in positive ways. A large number of people say that it originates with a deep spiritual focus, which comes from knowing that there is a greater power giving them purpose, hope and joy. When faced with difficult situations, prayer and meditation assist in reducing fear and anxiety. Several spoke about the security that comes with having a general sense of well-being, and good physical and mental health so that they can enjoy the present and plan for the future. To others, it had to do with having a positive, thankful attitude to counteract the negativity around them, or trusting their abilities to make good decisions, rather than continually second-guessing themselves. Why is peace of mind important to your true wealth? It enables you to forget about yourself and concentrate on the others you are with, again being completely present in the moment.

How Does True Wealth Impact Presence?

It is possible to have an empowered presence without money. The ABCs of image that we will be looking at in depth later – appearance, behaviour and communication – can make you very memorable. For instance, you don't need an expensive suit to have presence because your inner confidence will always be seen in your walk and posture. Showing civility and consideration for others, rather than being self-absorbed, can add to your charisma. As well, it is possible for everyone to be fully engaged, making the person you are with feel like the conversation you're having with them is the only thing matters at that moment.

When I think about having an empowered presence, I'm reminded of my wedding day over thirty years ago. After the ceremony, we had a cocktail reception at an historic property in an area of Toronto called Cabbagetown. It used to be one of the poorest communities in the city but gradually the dilapidated homes and warehouses were renovated to make room for 'yuppies' – young urban professionals. Alongside these upwardly mobile move-ins, the neighbourhood still had a mix of people with low incomes.

As photographs were being taken in the adjacent park, guests with champagne in hand spilled out of the hall to watch. A man dressed in a threadbare jacket who was not an invited guest, but likely a regular visitor to the park, approached the bartender and asked for a drink to toast the bride. After quietly raising his glass and enjoying the bubbly, he went off down the alley dancing a jig in my honour. He didn't need a good suit of clothes to attend our reception, and he certainly knew how to behave at this formal occasion. Most importantly, although he didn't know us personally, his total abandonment and joy added greatly to the celebrations of the day. Of all the guests that attended, I remember him the most.

Although it takes time to build, true wealth is not connected to age, gender, or economics. When you enjoy meaningful relationships, are fully engaged with life, and have peace of mind, you have nothing to gain by monopolising people or situations. When you show goodwill and empathy, people will gravitate closer, embrace the gifts they have, and share them with you. In turn, they too will experience the true wealth that comes with an empowered presence.

In the next few chapters, we will examine the role that your personal brand and image play in increasing confidence and self-esteem. Knowing who you are, what makes you unique and how to communicate it to others will make you memorable, continually increasing your true wealth and presence.

Chapter 2 - At A Glance

Meaningful Relationships

There is great value associated with the ability to develop meaningful relationships and the empowered presence that comes from knowing you are looked up to and can be counted on. Everyone can take the initiative to reach out to people and encourage them, so that they will draw nearer, embrace the gifts they have, and share them with you, adding to your true wealth.

Being Fully Engaged with Life

Even if you are completely fatigued at the end of the day, there is an abundant joy and fulfillment that comes from using your vision, talents, and energy to make a positive impact on your life and that of others, whether through gaining education, collaborating at work, being involved in humanitarian efforts or interacting in social circles.

Peace of Mind

Peace of mind is very personal, and has to do with the harmony created when many things in your life come together in positive ways and you feel secure and confident. When you have peace of mind, you can forget about yourself, concentrate on others and be completely engaged in the moment, a sign of true wealth and presence.

Brand YOU!

In the severe economic downturn between 2008 and 2010, the world witnessed one of the largest re-branding exercises in history involving the North American auto industry. As stocks plummeted and customer loyalty diminished, a series of complex government-secured loans and guarantees bought the industry some time to change its ways. And change it did, because not only was the future of the auto industry at stake, but arguably the very stability of the North American and world economies. With fuel costs rising, companies turned their focus from large SUVs to building vehicles which consumers actually wanted. Higher quality, fuel-efficient models, and several innovative adaptations involving cutting-edge technologies, helped re-establish buyer confidence and increased sales. If the industry continues to deliver on their brand promises, their future prospects should be bright.

Branding is responsible for what we choose to purchase, the causes that we support and how we are perceived by others. In this chapter, we'll look at branding as it relates to products in the marketplace and top-of-mind awareness, and how the same principles can be applied to creating your own personal brand promise – what you have of value that you can be trusted to consistently deliver when interacting with people – something that is vitally important in empowering your presence.

First, let's turn to what typically happens in the grocery store when buying your favourite snack. Without a second thought, you grasp the package from the shelf and toss it into your shopping cart. You never stop to read the label. You don't even weigh the pros and cons of your choice against all the other products vying for your attention, unless you're having a party and need to ponder the quantity or perhaps whether to add some variety.

When you get home, you pour over the story on the back of the bag which you've read many times before, delaying the inevitable enjoyment of your first morsel for just a moment longer. You know what to expect regarding the taste, texture, aroma, and even how it should sound when you bite into it. It's always the same, time after time.

What makes this process so automatic? It doesn't happen by chance. When you first try a product, although you may not want to admit this, it's often in response to one of the 3000 brand messages that you're bombarded with daily. If it doesn't disappoint, you purchase it again, and if it continues to satisfy, it becomes your snack of choice and you'll begin to recommend it to others. When shopping, you immediately recognize the product from simply the colours and graphics on the package, or even where it is positioned in the store. If the product doesn't appear to be in its usual place, because you trust the brand, you'll go out of your way to look for it.

So much goes on behind the scenes to ensure that this happens. First the physical product is developed, and then it is tested to ensure that it appeals to consumers, and that the texture, colour and flavour are consistent across both sample and production lots. Following this, packaging is designed using attractive graphics, images and colours, and then finally, a full marketing campaign is rolled out to convince you that you need the product before you ever enter the store.

How does this branding process apply to you personally? It's necessary to have top-of-mind awareness with the people you meet in order to be successful and have more presence. When you make a good first impression with someone, you create an opportunity to earn their trust. When your ongoing actions are consistent with this first encounter, you continue to earn and build more trust, and this in turn is usually rewarded with enhanced, lasting relationships – at work, at home and in your closest friendships. People will take you at your word because they know what to expect from you. They'll even go out of their way to spend time with you and tell others about you. This process results in greater self-confidence, which in turn will impact your relationships, career, and your true wealth potential. The process that builds this type of top-of-mind awareness is what I'll refer to as "personal branding."

What is Branding?

Let us start with the definition of a "brand." "A brand is a customer experience represented by a collection of images and ideas; often, it refers to a symbol such as a name, logo, slogan, and design scheme."[1] If you look at the colour used in a product's logo and packaging, which is only one aspect of the design scheme, you'll find that they are carefully chosen because our minds are programmed to respond to colour in certain ways. For instance, the laundry detergent aisle in the grocery store is a sea of blue and orange. This is because psychologically, blue is associated with cleanliness and orange with dynamic energy, so together they convey the message of "industrial strength cleaning power." [2] Even before you try the product, you expect it to deal with the toughest stains, and with only one wash. The shape of the logo and any slogan that accompanies it further work to win you over.

Once a brand is developed, the next goal is to have consumers recognize it in the crowded marketplace. "Brand recognition and other reactions are created by the accumulation of experiences with the specific product or service, both directly relating to its use, and through the influence of advertising, design, and media commentary"[3] As you can see, branding goes far beyond the concrete product, to all that surrounds bringing it to market and your cumulative experience over time. For instance, once you've used the laundry detergent and see that it didn't disappoint, loyalty that includes a certain emotional attachment, is created. Keep in mind that in personal branding, emotional attachments are also created with others through positive interactions; however, because of the human factor, they're even more meaningful and profound, thus building powerful relationships that are indicative of true wealth.

Evidence of branding goes as far back as ancient Egypt where hot irons were used to mark cattle to prove livestock ownership.[4] Of course, almost everything

---

[1] Search Engine Marketing Professional Organization (SEMPO)'s combined glossaries: http://www.sempo.org/?page=glossary#b

[2] Morton, Jill, "Color and Branding: Color Design and Psychology for Branding," Colorcom, 2012 http://www.colormatters.com/color-and-marketing/color-and-branding

[3] Search Engine Marketing Professional Organization (SEMPO)'s combined glossaries: http://www.sempo.org/?page=glossary#b

[4] http://www.britishmuseum.org/explore/highlights/highlight_objects/aes/b/bronze_branding_iron.aspx

we purchase today has a brand associated with it, from utilitarian brands for household products that live up to the purposes for which they were designed, to luxury brands for high-end automobiles that go beyond the basics to promise multi-dimensional experiences.

When working as the head fashion designer for a Canadian manufacturer, we experienced a dramatic shift in the late 1970s and early 80s with regards to what retailers expected. Instead of purchasing our branded products, they demanded that we design specific items for them, label them with their store brand, and promise exclusivity. This prevented consumers from making price comparisons, so that they could charge more and then deep discount the products to draw people into the stores. Brand awareness was increased, along with customer loyalty, and of course, their bottom line.

In an effort to get more of the market share in 1978, one grocery chain introduced a "no name" brand. The products, which were placed in plain, bright yellow packages, offered significant savings over national brands. Their marketing was so brilliant that on the day the concept was introduced, one location had to close their doors at 10:30 a.m. to control the crowds, letting people in only as other customers left the store.[5] Although "no name" suggests an absence of any brand, it was really the birth of a new one. Because they were so successful in communicating the brand personality of this line – that it represented affordable, quality products – they were immediately rewarded with exceptional sales. Generic products continue their popularity today.

In addition to the basic elements that go into creating a brand, such as the name, logo, graphics, tag line, shapes, colours, sounds, scents, tastes, etc., I want to talk more about the psychological aspects that promote a certain brand image in the consumer's mind. This involves feelings, perceptions, experiences, beliefs, attitudes, etc.

For instance, when you think of a favourite automobile, what comes to mind? Dependability? Speed? Prestige? Affordability? Luxury? Your answer will depend upon your circumstances and personality. If you have a young family, safety, versatility, and size might be uppermost. Whereas, if you're a single person looking for some fun on the road, although safety should be

---

[5] http://www.loblaw.ca/English/About-Us/history/default.aspx

important, other emotions will probably drive your decision. Also, depending upon what "fun on the road" conjures up, you could be drawn to a flashy sports car, or perhaps to a fuel-efficient hybrid, roomy enough for your camping gear.

Companies go to great lengths to create a brand and then manage it. What's important in all of this is that each successful brand has a clear sense of their core value – their brand promise to you. It not only sets them apart from their competition, but this unique selling proposition guarantees that certain characteristics will be there. It is a promise of value that they would like you to experience each time you use or consume their product. They want to ensure that your experience will be what you have come to expect and that it will always be positive.

Just as companies focus on creating a brand and managing the consumer experience, personal branding is about having a clear understanding of your authentic inner self and what you have to offer to others, and then aligning your outward appearance, behaviour and communication so that your brand message is consistent with who you really are, enabling you to establish meaningful relationships on an emotional level. The exercises at the end of the next section will assist you with this personal branding process – *Brand YOU!*

Personal Branding

Personal branding is not just for celebrities who are always in the public eye, but for everyone who wants to have more presence. It's not about hiding behind a created persona, being someone others think you should be, or trying to be the same as the peers you want to impress. Not only would this be seen as dehumanizing, it would camouflage the exceptional individual that you are. If you're a good actor, you could play along with it for a while, but eventually it will lead to exhaustion and disappointment all around.

Being authentically you is at the core of personal branding. You need to clearly understand what your strengths, personality traits, values, and passions are and how these can bring value to others – your unique promise of value. Later, you will find that it also involves making a plan to communicate what differentiates you from others. When you showcase what you know and believe to be true about yourself, you'll have more presence and be far more successful and empowered.

This is very evident in the world of sports. Athletes are encouraged to identify and develop their skills and strengths and then use positive affirmations and the power of visualization to influence results. I know a former Olympic skier who told me that technically she was better than her teammate who won the gold medal. In her opinion, the reason that the winner was successful was because she was in a better competitive frame of mind - she believed that she could win and the results certainly supported that.

The first step in creating your personal brand and empowering your presence is to define the characteristics that differentiate you from others. Many people haven't given much thought to their individual qualities. Those who are just beginning to test the waters of life may use such a high-powered magnifying glass when looking at others around them, that in comparison, they believe that they have nothing to offer. Others have been crushed by devastating experiences so that they too see very little of value in themselves. Still others simply have not taken the time to articulate what makes them distinct.

It's important not to gloss over the remaining sections of this chapter, but to set a goal to work systematically through them. Why is that? People often go through life on auto-pilot and do quite well navigating through daily activities at a minimal level, but they could be so much more. If you want to empower your presence and build true wealth, take some time to complete the exercises that follow. They will not only increase your self-esteem, but will form the basis of developing your personal brand statement and aligning with it everything else about you and your environment, such as your appearance, body language, email, verbal communication, office, mode of transportation and even where you volunteer. To speed up the process, it might be helpful to enter the heading along with the word "list" into an online search engine to come up with several options from which to choose.

Strengths

People have a difficult time talking about their strengths, because it is often considered poor form – close to bragging – when you speak about them. I've conducted hundreds of mock interviews with graduating students. Regardless of their education level, when I asked what their strengths were, a moment of silence usually ensued, followed by either more painful silence, or a string of overused platitudes about being a good worker, having excellent communication skills, being a team player, etc. Perhaps, the word "strengths" conjures up an expectation of perfection that no one wants to promise, leaving them with little to say. I savour the rare moments when interviewees had pondered this beforehand and treated me to concrete examples of what made them viable candidates. With this awareness, comes great presence. Psychologically, it may be easier for you to think about your talents and gifts as you work through these questions:

1. **What things do you enjoy doing?** List activities that you are good at, look forward to, do frequently, and experience a real sense of accomplishment when they're completed. Think about what you do in your personal, professional and social environments. Don't colour your responses with, "What would other people think if I included this?"

2. **What do others say you enjoy?** Ask your friends, family, supervisors, managers, coaches, teachers, mentors, etc. what they think you enjoy doing, what you are good at, and when they see you in your element.

3. **What are the common themes?** Examine the two lists and record the common features, plus anything else in the second list that you forgot to include that you think applies to you.

What did you learn about yourself from others? Hearing about your positive characteristics from a wide variety of people is instrumental in empowering your presence because it usually confirms what you instinctively know, but find hard to fully embrace.

Personality Traits

Your personality traits have to do with your innate qualities that are obvious to people around you. Your family would have noticed some of them long before you began speaking, while others were developed over the years. I have a great sense of humour. When I recently examined a photograph of me at age two, I could see the same mischievous smile that comes over my face today when I'm teasing someone or telling a funny story to illustrate a point in a seminar. Personality traits can include these four areas: your personal style, attitude, interpersonal skills, and work habits.

1. **Personal style:** List the words that describe your personal style. Are you assertive, responsible, flexible, etc.?

2. **Attitude:** List the words that describe your attitude towards life and other people. Are you positive, caring, open, etc?

3. **Interpersonal skills:** List the words that describe the way you interact and communicate with others. Are you tactful, cooperative, competitive, etc.?

4. **Work habits:** List the words that describe how you work. Are you decisive, resourceful, organized, etc.?

Look over your responses and highlight two or three key words in each section. Remember, to use these later to develop a clear personal brand statement. You'll need to choose things that authentically describe you.

Values

Values are standards, philosophies, principles and priorities which ideally guide your attitude, decisions, and actions. List 20 things that direct your life, work and relationships such as belonging, excitement, harmony, service, integrity, etc., and then narrow it down to your three most important values.

1.

2.

3.

Do these values guide your decisions? Would you associate them with having more presence? Do they align with what you see as true wealth? Hopefully, your values are in harmony with your reality or you may need to make some changes. For instance, if you value creativity over money and are in a job that gives you financial stability but leaves you little time for artistic pursuits, you're not going to be happy. Can you compromise in any way and still feed yourself? If you enjoy collaboration with people but have agreed to some volunteer work where you will be totally on your own, you may want to find a way to involve others.

Passions

You can't borrow passion. It involves a strong desire and enthusiasm that comes from deep inside you, and thus has the potential to motivate you in meaningful directions. Passions, when acted upon, can give you true joy. Although your pursuits may involve a lot of energy and strength (like anything worth doing), when you are passionate, it takes little effort to get you going. When you're doing something you love, you can get completely lost in the activity, lose track of time, and even set aside practical thoughts such as stopping for meals.

These questions will assist you in defining the passions that drive you: What social causes continually excite you? What gives you meaning in life? What makes you feel fulfilled? What activities do you get lost in? What actions empower you? What work or activity would you miss terribly if you ceased to do it? List your top three passions here:

1.

2.

3.

If you are having difficulty narrowing things down, check to see if there are any passions that span several areas of your life. Are there any that consistently drive you when interacting with people in your family, professional environment, educational pursuits, philanthropic work, social activities, etc? These tell you more about what compels you to be authentically you.

Your Key Personal Brand Elements

As previously mentioned, just as a company works to develop the basic brand elements of a product, such as the name, logo, colours, etc., the next step is to isolate your personal five key branding words. Look through what you've recorded in each area and highlight words that come up more than once and anything that especially speaks of you. It might be that you see certain talents, attitudes or skills used often when following your passions. Do any of them line up with the master list of the common characteristics that you admire in people with presence that you created in Chapter 1? That would be a bonus because these are things that you admire and probably hope to emulate in your own life, and they are already there. Don't worry about limiting yourself. Just as the automotive industry had to change gears to continue to be successful, these brand elements are yours for the moment and they may change over time as you grow and encounter new things in life.

1.

2.

3.

4.

5.

Developing a Personal Brand Statement

Now that you have identified your five key personal brand elements, I will describe how to create a personal brand statement that expresses your unique promise of value – what makes you stand out and what people will experience when they interact with you. This could be for a professional, volunteer or social context, depending upon your circumstances. The statement can be used when you are given 30 to 60 seconds to introduce yourself at a networking breakfast, board meeting, etc. It is also essential to develop because it will guide you as you bring everything else "on brand" – your image, resume, professional bio, online presence, office, marketing materials, philanthropic activities, etc.

To create a personal brand statement, start with your top personal brand elements. If you are in business, add a description of your client base and what makes you different from your competition. Now put them all together in one or two sentences that encapsulate who you are and what people can expect when working with you. The following is an example that uses information from a financial advisor:

Strength: Love numbers

Personality: Attentive listener

Values: Honesty, integrity

Passion: Help people achieve financial peace of mind

Client Profile: People who are worried about their financial futures

Competitive edge: 25 years experience in the financial markets

Personal Brand Statement: "After carefully listening to my clients, I use my love of figures and 25 years experience in the financial sector to prepare an honest analysis of their financial affairs. Then, together we carefully integrate their lifestyle, income, and retirement goals into achievable plans so that they will have financial peace of mind."

Notice that this personal brand statement didn't include a long list of services or products. Until the person you are talking to knows why they should listen, these details will be of little interest. It is more important to emphasize the values or benefits you bring to your clients.

Self-introduction

You will also need a shorter self-introduction to quickly capture people's attention in an elevator, at a business mixer, or when socializing. Here is an example for the same financial advisor:

> "My passion is to help my clients achieve financial peace of
> mind so that they can enjoy life to the fullest."

Self-introductions will vary in length and content, depending on the environment in which you find yourself and what you want to achieve. It is quite likely that you will need to develop several versions. Another reason to create a variety is that if you have invested the money to join a networking group that meets weekly, or even monthly, and you continually introduce yourself with the same infomercial, people will cease to listen. You will be passing up vital marketing opportunities. Lastly, notice how the phrase "financial advisor" was not included in either the personal brand statement or the self-introduction. I've been told by professionals in the industry that as soon as they say they are a financial advisor or tax specialist that conversations shut down pretty quickly – much like when I tell people I'm an image consultant. Again, concentrating on the benefits and values will be more effective in capturing attention.

As we continue on through the next chapters, you will learn how to align your image, environment and activities with your personal brand elements, so that you will always be presenting your authentic self and conveying your true value to others. When your personality, strengths, and values line up with your passions, and you begin to live your life with this knowledge, you will be amazed at how experiencing true wealth and an empowered presence are within your reach. In the next chapter, I'll take a closer look at what image is and how it plays another key role in communicating your intrinsic value and building true wealth.

Chapter 3 - At A Glance

Develop an Authentic Personal Brand

Just as companies focus on creating a brand and manage the consumer experience, personal branding is about having a clear understanding of your authentic inner self and what you have to offer others, and then aligning your outward appearance, behaviour and communication so that your brand message is consistent with who you really are.

Articulate Your Brand Essence

When you line up your strengths, personality traits, and values with your passions, and showcase what you know and believe to be true about yourself through your personal brand statement, you will be amazed at how true wealth and an empowered presence will be within your reach.

Provide a Consistent Brand Experience

When people continually have positive experiences when interacting with you, and trust you to consistently bring value to their lives, emotional attachments develop. This brand experience is responsible for building powerful relationships that are indicative of true wealth.

CHAPTER 4

Image Impacts Your Intrinsic Value

I had the opportunity to be a guest on CBC Radio, Canada's public broadcaster, for several Workology shows that explored the world of work, with topics ranging from the serious to the humorous. In preparation for a dining etiquette segment, Shelagh Rogers was asked to join us for lunch at a trendy Toronto bistro. I was thrilled because for many years, I'd heard Shelagh interviewing authors and enjoyed her warm, engaging style. At the same time, I was anxious because she was such a well known, respected radio host. When I arrived at the restaurant, Shelagh was standing in the vestibule with her back towards me speaking on her cell phone. When she completed the call, I cautiously approached her, and timidly asked, "Shelagh Rogers?" She swung around abruptly and began clutching different parts of her clothing, saying to me, "Catherine, I'm so nervous to meet you! And look at the awful shoes that I have on. I fell last week and have to be careful." I confessed that I felt the same uneasiness about our encounter, and immediately showed her my sensible shoes that I wear due to the late effects of polio. In that moment of candor, we both saw each other as people, so that we could relax and focus on the purpose of our meeting, which was the program.

Shelagh's reaction is typical of what often happens whenever someone discovers that I'm an image consultant. I've heard so many excuses as to why people are not dressed appropriately that I could write a book. We don't tell a plumber how to fix a leaky pipe, or our accountant how to file our income tax. We trust the expertise of these professionals.

Why will people readily use the skills of a mechanic, doctor or lawyer, but when it comes to their image, they are embarrassed to ask for expert assistance? What is it about one's personal image that evokes such an extreme level of self-consciousness? Why do some people give so little attention to their image, when others will assume so much about them based on their first impressions? I don't have all the answers to these questions. However, I do know that over the years, movies involving makeovers like *My Fair Lady*, or reality TV shows such as *What Not to Wear, Style by Jury, Extreme Makeover,* and so many more, captivate viewers. Obviously, there is interest in knowing how to transform one's image, and besides, it's something that everyone, to a certain degree, can do.

Research has shown that paying attention to your image can increase your self-esteem and confidence, adding to your success in life.[1] It's also one of the most powerful strategies you can use to communicate the essence of your personal brand to others, adding to your presence and true wealth. In this chapter, my goal is to dispel the mystery that surrounds the image profession by outlining what image is, as it relates to the person, why it's important throughout life, and what's involved in a typical image assessment when working with an experienced image professional.

The Difference between Fashion and Image

So many people confuse image with fashion and they are quite different. Fashion will get you ready for a date; your image prepares you for life. Having spent over 20 years as a fashion designer and educator, attending numerous functions and travelling extensively to source trends, I can confidently say that fashion is more about the end product rather than the wearer. Granted, as a designer, I enjoyed choosing the season's colours, creating visually pleasing garments, and teaching others how to do the same, but in fashion there's always a sense that if you don't wear the latest trends, you are somehow inferior.

When focussing on your image, although you need to be aware of trends, fashion takes a back seat to establishing your personal style. This is done by making informed choices gained from personal experience, research, or

---

[1] Linrud, Ph.D, Jo Ann K, AICI (Association of Image Consultants International Image) Study, Central Michigan University, August 2004

through engaging an image professional to assist. Instead of blindly adopting the season's styles, image has to do with choosing appropriate clothes that suit your individuality, personal colouring and physique. Expressing your personality in this manner can take you into a variety of situations with confidence, all the while communicating your true value to others.

My first introduction to the image sector was at an Association of Image Consultants International gala. Given my earlier description of how people worry about what they're wearing when meeting image consultants, choosing my outfit that evening was more difficult than with any other fashion event I'd attended. I felt that image consultants were hypercritical and with so many of them in one place, I expected to be severely judged. My concern soon vanished because what I found both surprised and pleased me. The room was filled with impeccably turned out professionals, buzzing with excitement as they warmly greeted one another and welcomed me into their circle. I remarked at how friendly everyone was compared to the people I met at numerous fashion functions I'd attended over the years. A seasoned professional turned to me and summed it all up with: "Of course, as image consultants our job is to help people be their best and we need to be approachable."

What is Image?

Image has to do with all that you project, consciously and subconsciously, through your appearance, behaviour and communication. It's a bundle of elements that provides others with an impression of you. People think that their image is tied solely to their external appearance; however, it has to do with understanding what is naturally deep inside you and revealing it to the outside world. Of course perception and reality are not always in sync, and in order for you to live authentically, they need to be aligned.

To illustrate this point, I'd like to share a story about a woman who planned to visit a networking group in order to see if it would be a good vehicle for expanding her business. Even though she had years of experience in sales, I was worried that her abrupt, dismissive attitude would create negative impressions and harm the development of relationships that are essential for generating referrals. Knowing that she'd be looking for an immediate return on her investment, I tactfully mentioned my concern to her. She was surprised, because she thought she came across as warm and caring. I soon showed her how to convey these positive traits using voice and body language, and suggested that she wear a mid-toned suit to make her appear approachable so that she would be positively received. These basic changes worked to her advantage.

Given that even experienced professionals are not aware of the impact of their first impressions on others, it's valuable to enlist the services of, an impartial friend, stylist or trained image consultant to find out if you come across in the way that you intend. It is not about having the right or wrong image because you are unique, but whether your image conveys your best traits and personality to others.

Why is Your Image Important?

Your image is very powerful because it can positively influence first impressions, which are almost impossible to change once they are formed. If you arrive late for a meeting with someone that you've never met before, and begin to blame the traffic, the potholes in the road, or a car that almost rear-ended you, this person will take what they experience in this first meeting at face value and fill in the blanks. They may decide that you have poor time management skills and are a complainer. From then on, they'll view you through a filter coloured by these assumptions. Each time you encounter that person again, this filter is activated. I realize that most reasonable people will be gracious if you're late, but some aren't and even if they are, these faux pas tend to stick in one's mind.

The lead author of a 2011 study on the persistence of first impressions[2], Bertram Gawronski, did share a small glimmer of hope regarding negative impressions. If after making a bad impression in one setting, you meet the person a second time in a new environment and have a positive experience, this new experience becomes "bound" to the context in which it was made.

For example, if you make a bad impression on someone in a social context and then that person encounters you in a professional environment and has a positive reaction, the person will think more positively of you in professional settings, but still won't want to socialize with you. Although first impressions are notoriously persistent, Gawronski notes they can sometimes be changed.

---

[2] Nauert Ph.D, Rick, "Why First Impressions Are Difficult to Change: Study," February 2011, http://www.livescience.com/10429-impressions-difficult-change-study.html

"What is necessary is for the first impression to be challenged in multiple different contexts. In that case, new experiences become decontextualized and the first impression will slowly lose its power," he said. "But, as long as a first impression is challenged only within the same context, you can do whatever you want. The first impression will dominate regardless of how often it is contradicted by new experiences."

Seeing that you will be judged, no matter what, think of the time and energy you'll save by making good impressions, and more importantly, the positive influences your presence will have on developing relationships with others. People will take you more seriously, listen to your ideas, and trust that you can add value. If you care about the way that you look, others will think that you care about your work. This can help in gaining employment, receiving promotions, obtaining new business, increasing client loyalty, and being entrusted with leadership roles. I'm not suggesting that you be vain and self obsessed, which is rooted in insecurity, but that you develop your own sense of personal style. This will increase your self-esteem and confidence and give you instant credibility with others.

Your image can be created and altered at any time, and it can be influential at all stages of your life, contributing to your true wealth. When transitioning from being a student to the competitive job market, a polished image can give you more presence, so that you will be seen as a prime candidate who could potentially bring value to the hiring organization. This can work at any age.

A mature law student seeking an articling position in an extremely competitive field contacted me because she had experienced obvious age discrimination and was preparing for a series of interviews. Because her budget was tight, I taught her how to use her existing wardrobe to create authoritative business attire that would span a number of interviews. She then learned how to confidently work a room, because she and a number of other interviewees had to attend a social hour hosted by the firm before the final interview candidates would be chosen. My client later called to say how empowered she was during the cocktail party, and more importantly, that she obtained the only position open in her area of practice.

An image update can also counteract feelings of being out of touch when re-entering the workforce after taking time off to raise children or care for a family member. When seeking a promotion or volunteering for projects that will require more responsibility, you'll be more successful when your image is aligned with what's expected. A competitor who doesn't pay any attention to their image will also be noticed, but for all the wrong reasons. Because managers find conversations surrounding image very uncomfortable, when two candidates have similar skills, it's always easier to promote the person with a polished image instead of spending resources on bringing someone up to the standard required for the position.

If you're a woman in a senior executive position, it is not surprising that statistics show that you'll be in the minority[3]. However, at the same time, you'll be highly visible, so a refined image can be one of your greatest assets to further your influence and continued advancement. If you're a self-employed entrepreneur starting out in your business, you'll not regret the investment in image coaching when it results in building client trust. Even if you've just retired or are experiencing changes in marital status or living arrangements, consider how an image update could assist with confidence and the development of relationships when navigating in new social circles.

Your Image and Personal Branding

Just like products vie for position in a noisy marketplace, you want to stand out, be recognized and trusted to deliver. Your image plays a role in this. When a new product is branded, a detailed marketing program is rolled out to capture customer attention, both at the visual and subconscious levels. In the same way, your image and personal brand can mediate the value judgements that are made about you when meeting people. Similar to a luxury brand that promises a consistently positive experience, you'll want to ensure that what people encounter when they interact with you is the same, time after time. This dependability helps you establish credibility, empowering your presence.

How do you do this? The key to increasing your presence comes from knowing what you want to publically say about yourself through your image, because a defined image that is purposeful and not left to chance, is one that successfully conveys the message that you intend. The good news is that you've

---

[3] http://www.calvert.com/newsArticle.html?article=20288

already decided what this message should be when you defined your five personal brand elements through the exercises in Chapter 3.

Once you know what you want to convey to others, you can develop specific image strategies to support these strengths, values, personality traits and passions that culminate in your unique promise of value. Remember, that you have at your disposal all the ABCs of image – appearance, behaviour and communication. Here is an example of how you can use all of them to ensure that your message is unified. If one of your passions is to help economically challenged people find employment, consider these tactics:

Appearance: Instead of wearing a dark coloured, highly constructed power suit, choose garments that make you appear approachable, such as a pair of slacks and a shirt. If a jacket is necessary, one that's in contrast to your pant or skirt would be best because you'll be less intimidating. You'll find out more about what I call the "ladder of formality" in Chapter 5.

Behaviour: Make it a priority to spend time with the people you want to assist so that you will fully understand their situations, rather than continually cancelling appointments at the last minute due to other commitments.

Communication: Match your voice and language style with that of the person you're speaking to, instead of sounding superior or talking down to them.

Of course there may be other strategies you'd be wise to employ. For instance, in order to reach your goal, you may need to contact organisations to ask for assistance with mentoring, job shadowing or internships. When interacting with business owners or human resources managers, adding a jacket to your attire will give you more presence, so that your request will be taken seriously. There are many more image strategies that will be discussed later in the book that you can use to influence situations, develop relationships, and achieve your goals.

How Can an Image Consultant Assist?
An image consultant is a mentor, a guide, a mirror, and a partner, who will help you identify your assets and challenges, and establish a public persona that will support you in reaching your full potential. Consultants recognize and appreciate your individuality and will make suggestions only after carefully listening to you, so that they will be in line with how you want to be

perceived and suitable for the contexts in which you find yourself. Image consultants who are generalists can assist you with your appearance, behaviour and communication, while others specialize in just one area and will refer you on to other skilled people when necessary.

It is important to ask about a consultant's credentials before engaging one because anyone can call themselves an image consultant. Although there isn't a single governing body that oversees the profession on a global level, there are excellent associations connected to the industry, such as the Association of Image Consultants International (AICI)[4], which require members to adhere to strict codes of ethics and professional standards. AICI also provides consultants with opportunities to be certified at three levels, and like the insurance and financial industries, they stipulate that certified members take ongoing educational training to maintain their certification.

Unlike many of the makeover shows, an image professional will not grab you and make you into something that you're not. Before any image goals are defined, an initial consultation is done. It usually involves a series of questions designed to fully understand what you hope to achieve by working with a consultant, such as what you want to say through your image, how you think you are currently perceived, whether you're facing new challenges in your life, how a change in your image could impact your presence, etc. The consultant will then tell you if your image is communicating what you think it is or whether it is working against you. Together you can then make a plan for further work which could include one or more services, such as identifying suitable colours and clothing styles, creating a wardrobe plan and budget, purchasing clothing and accessories, learning about business and social etiquette, enhancing your non-verbal and verbal communication skills, working a room with ease, delivering powerful presentations, preparing for an interview, and much more.

Your image is not set in stone. As circumstances in your life change, it is good to review your image goals, because what you wish to express through your public persona can also shift over time. You'll want to ensure that everything is in harmony. When you have a well-defined image in line with your personal brand that conveys the message you intend, you have the power to captivate and hold the attention of others, which is really what presence is all about.

---

4 http://www.aici.org

Image is Built from the Inside Out
The key to increasing your presence comes from knowing what you want to publically convey about your inner self through your outward image, because a defined image that is purposeful and not left to chance, is one that successfully transmits the message that you intend.

Managing Your Image Increases Confidence
Paying attention to your image increases your self-esteem and confidence, contributing to your success in life. Working with an image consultant who is a mentor, a guide, a mirror, and a partner, can help you identify your assets and challenges, and establish a public persona that will support you in reaching your full potential. Their goal is to help you be your best so that you can experience presence and true wealth.

Align Your Image with Your Brand
When you have a well-defined image in line with your personal brand that conveys the message you intend, you have the power to captivate and hold the attention of others, which is really what presence is all about. To achieve this, use all the ABCs of image: appearance, behaviour, communication.

Your Platinum Edge: Appearance

I was invited to speak to a university business class about the importance of image in sales and marketing. Soon after, one of the students who had been hired by an information technology giant emailed, "Am I too young to have an image consultant?" He had just completed ten months of training at their headquarters and was returning to Canada to assume a sales management position. I told him that seeking guidance so early was a smart strategy because his image would assist him with what he wanted to achieve professionally. We did an initial consultation to define his image goals, challenges, work environment, successes, client demographics, and the message he wanted to convey to others. His biggest concerns were his young age and lack of experience. He knew, compared to other firms, his company's technological solutions were far superior, but his competitor's salespeople were much more seasoned than he was. After defining his personal brand message and identify his most suitable garment details, together we purchased a wardrobe that would take him from the boardroom to the golf course. The next week, he told me how pleased he was because our work had done so much to increase his confidence during his very first sales call.

After many years in the image business, I'm continually astonished when I see that focusing some attention on one's own image can be so influential in increasing confidence. It is equally remarkable that many don't take their image seriously, and in fact, often equate work in this area as simply playing with clothes – fluff. What if you could harness the power of your image to support your brand message and increase your personal and professional success? As we look at the ABCs of image – appearance, behaviour and communication – I'll show you many strategies that will give you the necessary edge to be successful in your career and personal life, which will positively impact your true wealth and presence.

Why is Appearance so Important?

Our society is so visual that your appearance will always make a statement, even if you don't wish it to. Your appearance is an outward expression of your inner essence; therefore, what people see on the outside, needs to be in sync with your authentic self, and work for you, not against you. If you are confident in your appearance, you'll attract the attention of clients, friends, employers, potential life partners, team leaders, constituents, etc. Even if you are naturally reserved, your appearance can help you command more attention when you walk into a room filled with strangers; when you open your mouth, people will listen to you. Also, if you have a cultural or language challenge, when words fail you, your appearance can compensate, communicating what you intend. I think you'll agree that although your appearance will never make up for a lack of ability, it will influence people's assumptions and behaviour, affecting ultimate outcomes.

Attractiveness

Appearance involves far more than simply being physically appealing to others. However, studies do show that physical attractiveness can impact our relationships and success. I'm not talking about the sexual attractiveness that a beautiful woman or a buff fellow might have, but how your physical features will cause people to make decisions about you before you have any meaningful contact with them. A study that focused on how facial features were used to judge attractiveness, likeability, trustworthiness, competence and aggressiveness, concluded that people draw trait inferences from facial features within a mere tenth of a second.[1] Think about it - just a tenth of a second!

People pay closer attention to attractive people and are able to identify their personality traits more accurately compared to judgments involving less at-

---

[1] Willis, Janine & Todorov, Alexander, "First Impressions: Making Up Your Mind After a 100-Ms Exposure to a Face," Association for Psychological Science, 2006, http://psych.princeton.edu/psychology/research/todorov/pdf/Willis&Todorov-PsychScience.pdf

tractive people,[2] implying that attractive people have a natural magnetism which holds attention longer. As well, attractive people are seen to be more intelligent, socially competent and emotionally stable (although not as more considerate). In addition, attractive people do better financially because they are hired sooner, get promotions more quickly and are often paid more than less attractive co-workers.[3]

Although the judgments of people's faces are usually very accurate, even when they are not, the impressions made are so consequential because they lead us to assume and attribute characteristics and dispositions to people that ultimately affect their success and opportunities.[4] For example, when teachers believed that attractive children had more potential than unattractive children, it substantially impacted their actual academic success.

Facial maturity also influences impressions. Adults who have a babyish face (e.g., a large forehead, high eyebrows, large eyes, non-prominent cheekbones, and a small jaw) are often believed to be submissive, naïve, weak, warm and honest – that might be helpful if you're in court. In contrast, mature-faced persons (e.g., a small forehead, a heavy brow ridge, prominent cheekbones, and a large jaw) are often seen as dominant, shrewd, powerful, competent and untrustworthy.

Even though your facial features are a given, short of having plastic surgery, which I'm certainly not suggesting, you can still use your face to immediately connect with others by smiling. Our brains are hardwired to respond to a person we initially meet in one of four ways: friend, enemy, sexual opportunity or indifference. Of course when you smile, you'll be seen as a friend and everyone can relax. If you also raise your eyebrows, the message will change from "friend" to "family."[5] Later in the book, I will talk more about

2   Nauert, Ph.D., "First Impressions of Attractive People More Accurate," University of British Columbia, 2010, http://psychcentral.com/news/2010/12/22/first-impressions-of-attractive-people-more-accurate/22059.html

3   Maestripieri, Ph.D., Dario, "The truth about why beautiful people are more successful," *Psychology Today*, 2012, http://www.psychologytoday.com/blog/games-primates-play/201203/the-truth-about-why-beautiful-people-are-more-successful

4   https://tspace.library.utoronto.ca/bitstream/1807/33142/1/Rule&Ambady%282010_SPPC%29.pdf

5   Bowden, Mark, *Winning Body Language for Sales Professionals: Control the Conversation, Command Attention, and Convey the Right Message without Saying a Word*, McGraw Hill, 2013

non-verbal communication and how it can help you to create trust and good rapport with people. For now, we'll continue to focus on other components of appearance.

Does Your Appearance Support Your Brand?

Your "brand" is connected to what people see and think of you. Just like packaging supports a product and its brand message, your clothing, accessories and grooming need to do the same for you. I once encountered a person selling expensive nutritional supplements at a tradeshow, who undoubtedly missed many opportunities that day because of his image. Although his booth was attractive, his appearance totally undermined his message. He needed a haircut and a shave, his shorts were far too casual for the venue, his t-shirt didn't quite cover his stomach, and his running shoes were filthy – not an image most people would associate with wellness.

Your image needs to be an asset, rather than a liability. If you like yourself and love what you do, show it through your appearance and others will be attracted to you. Be consistent with everything connected to your appearance, because even after making a good first impression, you want to appear responsible, living up to the expectations that others have of you and your brand.

Clothing

Throughout history, clothing has been an indicator of one's occupation, position in society and economic status, whether through starched lace collars requiring a staff to maintain them, prestigious university ties, or the latest designer labels. In Western society, we usually have complete freedom when it comes to what we wear, so factors that affect wardrobe choices are mainly influenced by personality, lifestyle, individuality, and if applicable, work environment. They might also be further guided by personal beliefs, disabilities or physical sensitivities. Comfort should be your top priority when choosing garments. If you're completely comfortable in your attire and it is suitable for the occasion, you will feel secure and relaxed in your clothing and others will have confidence in you. You will be able to forget about yourself and focus totally on others – a sign of having true presence.

On the other hand, if you are uncomfortable in your clothes, you'll be distracted and your confidence and presence will be undermined. Equally important is whether your attire makes others feel ill at ease. If your suit is too formal and intimidating, the amount of skin exposed is provocative, or if you convey a lack of respect by dressing inappropriately for the occasion, your appearance could impede the sort of connection that is necessary to establish meaningful relationships.

In all of this, clothing and accessories should never disguise your true self. Asking questions such as these before you leave your closet will avoid this happening. Do they express my personality? Do they help people see who I am and what I'm capable of? Do they enhance my best features? Do I feel confident? As we examine clothes at work, there will be other questions you'll need to ask yourself, so that the image you project is truly the one you intend.

Clothes at Work

In my experience, many people have not made the important connection between their image and their earning potential. A confident appearance that is in sync with your work culture can only help to increase your career options. When deciding what to wear, start with defining what is considered appropriate. Every organization has a dress code, whether written or implied, that is suitable for their industry, geographic location and client base. If you're an owner or CEO of a company, having a clearly defined dress code will ensure that employees will know what is expected in order to support your company brand at all times. As a potential employee or service provider, until you determine a firm's clothing guidelines, it's always safer to dress more formally than appearing too casual.

Once inside, dress as well as your peers, and if you want to have more presence, slightly better than they do. Besides, if you dress for the position that you want, assuming that you possess the necessary skills, you'll often be considered for promotion ahead of others who don't look the part. As well in a competitive marketplace, if your appearance tends to be more laid back, people might not trust that you have the necessary ability to handle certain responsibilities; however, for a position that requires you to be approachable and caring a less structured look might be perfect. If you are a manager who wants to have more presence to inspire your team, dress more formally than your staff. At times, the absence of a jacket can also work to your advantage – it's all about strategy. For instance, if you need to create more rapport with your staff, you could remove your jacket before meeting with them in order to open up communication.

Sometimes people worry about dressing better than their supervisors. This should not be a concern because a good supervisor won't be intimidated. First rate managers hire people whom they can count on as their representatives, and eventually to be their replacements when they decide to retire or are transferred to other areas.

Once you've established a reputation, be careful not to lose credibility by dressing down too far. This is especially true for women. When men dress down, they lose some authority; when women dress down, they seem to lose *all* authority. In the next section, you'll learn more about how to navigate various workplace environments with appropriate levels of professional and business casual attire, so that your appearance will always support you and empower your presence.

Demystifying Business Casual

In the technology boom of the 1990s, much of the workforce moved from wearing traditional business attire (consisting of a suit with a shirt and tie, or a blouse), to business casual attire, if not on a daily basis, at least on Fridays. However, relaxing dress codes raised several concerns. Many employees didn't understand what was appropriate for *business casual* dress. They arrived for work in tattered jeans, T-shirts emblazoned with lewd slogans, tank tops, short shorts and bra tops. In response, some companies rushed to put acceptable casual-dress guidelines into writing, and some even banned dressing down entirely, reverting back to formal business attire that was unequivocally understood. Other businesses insisted that employees who had direct contact with the public dress formally, while the rest who were not on the front lines could be casually attired.

Confusion about business casual attire still exists today. Some companies are now labelling it "business appropriate dress," and leaving employees to decide what is professional in each situation they encounter. Regardless, studies on whether casual attire influences productivity, employee engagement and client perceptions continue to be done. At times, it feels like we are dangling from the end of a pendulum, swinging back and forth, as each study contradicts the last. I don't believe that things will swing totally back to the "dress for success" era[6] of the 1970s and 80s. Some form of casual attire at work is here to stay for most industries. If you are in the financial sector, one thing to note is that the public is very critical when those handling their wealth dress down too much. I'll talk more about this in Chapter 9.

Also, when the economy is lack lustre and competition in the marketplace is high, if companies are equal in terms of what they offer, customers will fixate on what sets them apart. It could be their customer service, or their ability to connect with clients and instil confidence. Because clothing does play a role in this, especially in corporate environments, staff are often asked to dress up more. For instance, one financial institution where business casual attire was worn daily, instead of going all the way back to formal business attire, they simply asked the men to wear ties with their dress shirts and trousers.

Your first task in getting dressed should be to ask yourself a few more questions. How do I want to be perceived – knowledgeable, powerful, approachable? What do I want others to think about me – I'm professional, I'm fun, I'm knowledgeable? What will I be doing today – negotiating a contract, delivering a seminar, doing paperwork? Where will I be working – at a fundraiser, in a corporate office, in the field? What kind of response am I looking for – to be believed, trusted, or ignored?

Once you have a sense of what you'll be doing and what you want to achieve, then you can plan your wardrobe in a strategic way so that it supports your efforts. What is clear is that if you dress inappropriately, your goal to have more presence will be compromised, affecting your personal brand and true wealth. Let's look at the factors that make clothing seem more casual or more dressed up, so that you'll always be confident in your wardrobe communication.

The Ladder of Formality

Each context in which you find yourself may require you to wear different degrees of professional or casual dress. Understanding the five factors that affect the perceived formality or informality of your clothing will help you decide where you should be on the "ladder of formality." Dressing strategically will always strengthen your personal brand and add to your self-esteem and presence.

---

[6] http://www.thedressforsuccesscolumn.com/

1. **Clothing Layers:** The greater the number of clothing pieces worn at one time, the more formal you'll appear. For instance, a suit will be at the top of the ladder of formality, and a shirt and pants, or skirt, further down.

2. **Colour:** The darker your colours, the more powerful your look, especially when they are combined with high contrasting tones. (E.g. a navy suit with a white or ecru shirt.) Muted, traditional tones such as black, navy and grey are more formal than bright ones.

3. **Fabric:** The smother and plainer the fabric, the more formal it is. Woven fabrics will be further up the ladder than knits, and fine knits will appear more dressed up than textured ones. Wools, silks and microfibres are more polished than linens, cottons and blends, unless they are heavily textured. Florals and paisleys will make you more approachable, while fabrics that shine or cling are at the bottom of the professional scale.

4. **Tailoring:** The more tailored your clothing, the more presence you will have. For example, a soft, unlined jacket is not as strong as one with a lining, shoulder pads and interfacing. A long-sleeved garment will be further up the ladder than one with short sleeves.

5. **Accessories:** Finer accessories, such as shoes with thin soles, gold or silver jewellery, and leather portfolios, are more formal than heavier pieces in textured materials. Ensure that the level of formality of your clothes and accessories are similar.

A Guide for Dressing Down

In addition to the five factors that will move you up or down on the ladder of formality, the following will help decipher what professional attire is and when it is appropriate, and how to dress casually at three distinct levels. You don't want to bottom out when dressing down in the workplace, so your approach will depend on your work environment, who you will be meeting, and what you want to achieve.

Traditional Business Attire

When you desire to have a powerful presence, wear traditional business attire. It is authoritative and is typically worn when going to most job interviews, attending corporate meetings, delivering formal presentations, handling wealth, and negotiating with major clients. It includes a full suit (a structured jacket and matching pants or a skirt) worn with a dress shirt and tie for men, and a blouse or tailored shirt for women. Women can also wear a dress and jacket or a tailored coat dress. Fabrics are made from natural fibres or microfibers, and are plain, finely textured or subtly patterned in traditional, muted tones. Accessories are classic, understated and finely detailed.

Three Levels of Business Casual

Tailored Business Casual

This level has moderate authority and is worn on a "dress-down day" by managers or consultants who normally wear professional attire, staff dressing up to meet with management, and anyone expecting client contact in semi-casual environments. The key element at this level is a *tailored jacket*. It's usually worn with a contrasting pair of pants or skirt for a two tone look. A dress shirt and tie, open collared shirt, blouse, polo shirt, mock turtleneck, full turtleneck, crewneck or V-neck can be worn underneath. Fabrics will be generally fine and could include knits, cotton, linen, tweeds, and possibly leather and suede. Patterns can be bolder compared to those used in traditional attire.

Smart Business Casual

The smart business casual category is the most widely accepted. It is used when out of view of important clients, doing on-site consulting where business casual is the norm, and as a quality look for the information technology industry. This category is positioned in the middle of the ladder of formality and spans some distance with colour, fabrication, and accessories determining the level. The key element here for men is a *collared shirt* (including mock turtlenecks and full turtlenecks). At the top of this classification would be an outfit in traditional colours consisting of a dress shirt and a tie, worn with wool trousers and fine accessories. At the bottom would be a brightly coloured, short-sleeved, knitted polo shirt worn with cotton pants and thick-soled shoes.

The guidelines for women are not as clear, and the choices are as plentiful as the mistakes that can be easily made, especially at times when fashion trends include clothing that leaves little to the imagination. A collared shirt is not essential, but preferred if you want to stand out. Keep in mind the presence that comes through layering your clothing pieces, and think about a pulled-together outfit that includes three pieces. For example, instead of just wearing a pair of pants and a knit top, add a cardigan, unconstructed jacket or scarf to give you a more polished appearance.

Relaxed Business Casual

This level of dress has been adopted by people working mainly in information technology, artistic sectors, and the trades. Industries that generally dress more formally prefer that staff wear these garments on the weekend or at company picnics. Fabrics and colours can be combined in innovative ways, suggesting that the wearer is free-thinking, informal, creative and hard working; accessories are heavier and more textured. Instead of one key item, there are a number of fabrics and styles that are associated with this level that are not usually allowed in the upper two categories: denim (all colours), T-shirts, sleeveless garments, tank tops, strapless tops, shorts, fleece, running shoes and casual sandals. Studies done in the United States also included leather and suede on this list,[7] but in countries like Canada, they are more widely accepted. If there are any slogans on the clothing, companies prefer that it be their firm's logo, not that of your favourite beverage or sports team.

Personal Wardrobe Considerations

In addition to all the factors we've examined so far, there are also personal wardrobe considerations such as your clothing personality, what suits your skin tone, and how the style lines of your garments relate to your physique that impact how you look and feel in your clothing. Knowing something about your clothing personality will help you understand why one garment is more "you" than another, and possibly why you've never worn particular clothing gifts bestowed upon you by well-meaning friends and family. The four most common clothing personalities are Classic, Dramatic, Romantic and Natural. You'll usually find that your clothing will fit into one dominant category and that you also relate to one or more of the other styles.

In a working context, you may set your dominant personality aside if you think it could be a distraction or perhaps does not give you enough presence. For instance, a bank manager desiring a look of authority at work decided to

---

[7] Amiel, Ilene & Angie Michael, *Business Causal Made Easy: The complete guide to business casual dress for men and women, Business Casual Publications, Inc., 1999*

wear classically tailored suits, which carry a sense of power, instead of romantic floral dresses more suited to relaxed social functions.

Classic

The classic personality is drawn to traditional clothing styles that are simple, understated and conservative, such as formal business attire. The lines and textures of classic clothing are never extreme. Fabrics for ties and blouses are plain or in small or medium prints in traditional paisley patterns, polka dots, subtle checks, stripes and plaids in muted colour combinations. Everything is in moderation. A classic person can safely invest in high-quality pieces because classic garments are timeless.

Dramatic

Instead of conservative styles, the man or woman who is dramatic enjoys wearing garments that are striking, theatrical and creative. Dramatic people will wear the latest fashion trends, often with a structured, bold cut and a defined shoulder. Fabrics such as gabardines and smooth worsted wools will be stiffer, and prints and patterns will be in sharp, contrasting colours. Accessories are never inconspicuous, with jewellery having a sculptural quality, or it may be glamourous and glitzy. Ties will make a strong statement, or they'll be monochromatic. Dramatic people are never overlooked in a crowd.

Romantic

Someone who is romantic enjoys rich, luxurious clothing without the extremes of the dramatic person. Fabrics will be soft, fine and drape well, such as lightweight wools, challis, silk and buttery leather. Romantic women enjoy delicate floral prints, lace, ruffles and feminine colours. Romantic men are fashion-conscious, and their clothing has smooth, softly curved lines in rich, sometimes shimmering, fabrics. Accessories will include solid silk ties and simple, elegant jewellery. Everything is tasteful, soft and subtle.

Natural

The typical natural person enjoys casual, outdoorsy and informal clothing. If it's necessary to wear a jacket, it will always be sporty. The cut of the clothing, especially in menswear, will be fuller, giving a roomy, comfortable fit. Natural men will prefer sports jackets to structured suits. Natural women will prefer slacks to skirts. Fabrics will be textured and rustic such as corduroy, flannel and tweed, with colour combinations in harmony with the outdoors.

Nothing is shiny, fancy or too formal. For those who are natural, less is better than more.

Individual Colours and Style Lines

Using the colours and style lines of your clothing to enhance your best features is a science in itself. Knowing what suits you before purchasing any clothing will not only make you look incredible, but it will continue to build your confidence. You'll be able to easily make successful choices in the stores, saving you time, energy and most of all money.

You already know that colour can make you appear approachable or powerful, as seen with the ladder of formality. It also has the power to affect your emotions, the reactions of people around you, and your general appearance. Knowing whether your skin tone is cool, warm or neutral is important. When you're wearing colours that are in harmony with your skin, you'll look rested, younger, healthy and vibrant, while colours that are not the best, will make you appear tired, flushed or possibly jaundiced.

Your body is unique and perfect, even when popular culture suggests otherwise – that's another difference between image and fashion! Become comfortable with your physique and learn how to dress to accentuate your best features. If you'd like to draw attention away from a certain feature, or balance a particular area of your body, an image professional is trained in using the elements and principles of design to create harmony and lead the eye to your face. There are also many online tools available for men[8] or women[9] that can do a personal assessment of your physical characteristics and recommend your best clothing and accessory styles. Armed with information, you'll enjoy shopping because you'll take fewer items into the change room and know how to respond to, "That looks great!" if you think it doesn't. This is very empowering.

Establishing a Quality Image

After considering the appropriate formality strategy for your attire, the personal brand message you want to communicate, and your individual features and preferences, there are several other things connected to appearance that

---

[8] http://www.prime-impressions.menofstyle.com

[9] http://www.prime-impressions.myprivatestylist.com

will help you establish a quality image. No one regrets buying quality items because they will last longer, perform better and require less maintenance. If you're enticed to buy clothing based solely on price, the old adage, "You get what you pay for," usually holds true. Although something might cost more initially, purchasing quality will double or triple the life of the item. It is remarkable that when you do invest in an excellent wardrobe, that an insignificant detail can still interrupt the communication process. A button out of place, a tie that twists, or an overcoat that is too short—all these, and more, can create visual distractions.

Building a Wardrobe

You'll always reap great benefits from carefully planning your wardrobe instead of buying garments on the spur of the moment. These tips will help you get the most out of your wardrobe dollars.

- Just as you would invest in career training or upgrading your skills, allocating 1% of your annual income to your wardrobe is an effective guideline for wardrobe development and maintenance. If you're just starting out in your career, the information on wardrobe capsules later in this section will help extend what money you have.

- Take an inventory of your closet to see whether your garments suit your needs and whether they'll take you into the environments where you spend your time. Cull out pieces that you dislike, are dated, fit poorly, are stained or worn out, don't suit your current lifestyle, and haven't been worn in three years. Look over the remaining garments and take note of any that need cleaning, repairs, alterations, or replacement and commit to bringing them up to a wearable standard. Set aside any garments you are not sure about and make an appointment with an image consultant for their expert opinion, because sometimes all they need is a small alteration. If there are items you're hoping to shrink into, store them out of sight because guilt garments are never empowering. Make a shopping list of the accessories required to complete outfits, worn core items that need replacing, and new pieces that are necessary to address any lifestyle changes.

- Spend your clothing dollars where you spend your time because a garment that you don't wear, regardless of cost, is the most expensive piece in your closet. Be careful not to buy something you don't need just because it's on sale.

- If your budget is tight or you travel globally, aim to have at least 75% of your wardrobe in transitional fabrics, patterns and colours so that you can wear them ten to twelve months of the year.

- Choose timeless classics in traditional colours for the higher-investment items such as suits and coats, and then bring in some fashion colours with less expensive shirts, blouses, sweaters, ties and scarves. This strategy will help you maintain a contemporary look and will again maximize your clothing dollar.

- Garments made with quality fabrics and construction will always look and feel better. Although wool needs to be dry cleaned, it's worth the investment because wool garments will drape beautifully and last for years. Sea Island and Egyptian cotton will crease less than other varieties of cotton. Avoid purchasing garments with puckered seams because pressing can never make up for poor construction.

- Designer labels don't always mean that you are getting a higher quality garment. A man's suit made by a dependable, domestic manufacturer selling for $795.00 will usually be of better quality than one with a designer label at $1000.00. In order to get the same quality as the domestic product, the designer product would probably have to retail closer to $3000.00.

- Second-hand stores can be a source of high quality, gently used clothing at a fraction of its original cost. Check the fabric, construction and fit and compare it to the general style of the day. Altering will update some garments, but not all, and an item long past its era isn't a bargain at any price. Don't sacrifice your credibility for the sake of a few dollars.

- Accessorize a new outfit before leaving the store so that it is ready to wear.

- When combining different pieces in your wardrobe, although some textural contrast is interesting, it's safer to keep similar fabric textures together.

- When combining patterns, "less is more," so when wearing a suit, shirt and tie, always choose at least one piece in a plain fabric. For example, a pinstriped suit with a patterned tie would be best worn with a plain shirt. The colours should also coordinate. For instance, your tie should contain colours that are in your shirt or jacket. When up close, they don't have to match exactly, but they should appear to blend when looking at them from a distance.

- Exaggerated patterns and loud colours usually don't project an image of quality and garments using them will become dated quickly. If you want the excitement that they bring, use them sparingly in less expensive items or weekend wear.

- Pull together a wardrobe capsule, which is a small group of items in one or two colours that you can mix and match. Nine pieces of well-coordinated clothing will create 20 outfits. Developing your wardrobe in this manner reaps tremendous rewards. You will save money, (as well as the environment), packing a suitcase will be a breeze, and dressing will be easier. For example, if one garment is in the laundry, there will always be something else in your closet that you can wear in its place. Also, if you are visually impaired, you won't have to worry whether one garment goes with another.

Fit Guidelines

The fit of your garments is a reflection of quality. You can pay a large sum for a garment, but if you haven't taken the time to make sure it fits properly, it will look like an inexpensive piece. Many people who dislike shopping are notorious for rushing into a store, trying on a garment and leaving before it is properly checked for fit. Alterations do not mean that your body is problematic, but that the measurements used to create the ready-to-wear were not your measurements. We should expect to have some alterations if we want garments to fit well. Menswear stores usually include the price of most alterations in the cost of the clothes because they anticipate that some will be necessary; women's stores charge extra. Here are some things to watch for:

- Avoid clothing that is too tight or too loose.

- When choosing a suit or coat, the fit of the shoulders is your first priority. For a skirt or pant, fit the largest part of your body, and alter other areas as necessary.

- The collar of a woman's suit jacket should fit impeccably. It is much easier to make changes in men's collars because their suit jackets are constructed with alterations in mind. About .95 to 1.25 cm (3/8 to 1/4") of a man's shirt collar should be visible just above the back edge of the jacket collar.

- If you have an obvious posture challenge that affects the hang of your garments, or there is a large discrepancy between your upper and lower body, a garment may need to be made to measure. Sometimes you can order stock separates (a top of one size and a bottom in a different size).

- Your pants must be long enough. When wearing low shoes, they should end just above where the heel meets your shoe in the back and have a crease in the front, so that when you walk they don't ride up too far. When wearing wide pants with high heels, the bottom of the hem should come to the middle of your heel.

- Jackets are investment pieces. If the jacket is the wrong length, a good, balanced proportion will not be created. The length of the jacket is influenced by the jacket style and the relationship of your body and legs to your overall height. Advice from an experienced retailer, designer, tailor or image consultant will guide you in this matter.

- Sleeves shouldn't be too long or too short. Although sleeve length is a personal decision, jacket sleeves should usually come past your wrist bone to the first joint on your thumb; shirt sleeves should be .6 to 1.25 cm (1/4 to 1/2") longer.

- If you tuck in your shirts, they should be long enough to stay in place during normal movement. Any excess fabric at the waist can be removed by sewing vertical darts in the back.

- Before making a final purchasing decision, stand in front of a three-way mirror to see if the back of the garment hangs well. Also, check to make sure that your garments still cover your body and underwear when you bend over and reach up. If they don't, you'll not want to make that discovery later!

- Your outerwear really should be a priority instead of a last thought, because when the weather is cool, your coat is the first garment that people see. Men's full-length overcoats should come at least 5 to 7.5 cm (2 to 3") below the knee. If you prefer to wear a shorter coat, in order to fully cover your suit jacket, choose a three-quarter-length style rather than a bomber jacket. Women's full-length coats should come at least 5 to 7.5 cm (2 to 3") below the knee when you're wearing pants and the same amount below the hemline of a skirt or dress.

Accessories

Your accessories, and in particular your shoes, will tell others a lot about you, your priorities, and your attention to detail. A worn belt, an outdated cell phone, or a broken umbrella will never make a good impression; a quality pen is essential when writing up business.

Shoes

- Polish won't cover deep scuffs that are the result of inattention, so polish them regularly and repair heels before they've completely run down.
- Men's shoes can always be brown; otherwise they should either match or be darker than the colour of their trousers. Cordovan, a rich shade of burgundy, will also coordinate with a number of cool tones.
- A woman can match her shoes to her skin tone or hemline, or be darker. Closed-toed pumps with medium, tapered heels and sling-backs are always appropriate for business attire, while high stilettos are not. Open-toed shoes, sandals, and high fashion styles or colours are best for relaxed business casual attire.

Belts

- Men should match their belt to their shoes, unless they are casually attired or wish to make a fashion statement.
- Women can match their belt to their shoes, pants, skirt, or purse and also have fun with contrasting colours and textures.

Jewellery

- When dressed in formal business attire, women's jewellery should be discreet and of good quality. Wear no more than four pieces at once unless working in creative fields where dramatic individuality is usually expected.
- Men should be careful with wearing opulent pieces in business because they could intimidate and distract some people.

Eye Glasses

- Choose frames according to your personality and purpose because they can make you appear sophisticated, naïve, artistic, scholarly, authoritative, etc.
- Your frames should complement your face shape, brow line, placement and size of your eyes, length and size of your nose and personal colouring.

- Wearing tinted glasses indoors inhibit eye contact and could suggest that you're hiding something.

Fine-Tuning the Details: Men's and Women's Wear

Short-Sleeved Dress Shirts

- A long-sleeved dress shirt is always appropriate. If you're warm, roll your sleeves halfway to the elbow, but no further.
- A short-sleeved dress shirt worn with a tie doesn't project an image of quality.

Tight Shirt Collars

- A collar that is too tight becomes a distraction because excess flesh will spill over the top. Also, men's studies show that a tight collar actually cuts off blood circulation to the brain, affecting its function, causing dizziness and visual problems [10].

Button-Down Shirt Collars

- A button-down collared shirt should never be worn with a double-breasted jacket because it's too sporty. Shirts that have hidden snap or button closures beneath the collar points are a better choice.

Tie Tips

Your tie is a very important expression of your personality. Master all the possible knots, using one of the many online resources if necessary, and then follow these tips for using ties to your best advantage.

- Purchase good-quality ties that are fully lined. Hold the tie by the small end and see if it hangs straight. If it twists, it's not cut on the true bias, and it will always twist on your body.
- The widest part of your tie should be close to the width of the lapel on your jacket and the knot in proportion to the space between your collar points.
- Tie your tie so that the narrow end is shorter than the wide end and the point reaches the bottom of your belt buckle, then tuck the narrow end into the tab on the back. If it's too short, instead of tucking it into your shirt at the top, which creates a distraction, move the tab up further. There

---

[10] Gifford Jones, Dr. W., "The Tight Pants Syndrome!" Canada Free Press http://www.canadafreepress.com/medical/gastroenterology091095.htm

should always be one or more dimples at the base of the knot to help the tie spread and prevent it from collapsing.

- To make your tie last longer, untie it completely at the end of the day, instead of loosening the knot and slipping the tie over your head. If the tie has become excessively creased, place both ends together and roll the tie up as you would a belt. The creases will usually be gone by morning.

Men's Suit Jackets, Blazers and Trousers

- A suit jacket is cut a little tighter than a blazer or sports jacket, so if you try to wear it as if it was a blazer with contrasting trousers, it will look odd.

- If you regularly wear your suit trousers without the jacket, purchase two pairs of trousers or separate ones to wear with blazers and sports coats on business casual days. If your thighs are heavy have the crotch of your trousers reinforced.

- To prevent creasing, a double-breasted jacket should be buttoned when you're standing and unbuttoned when seated. *Never button the bottom button on vests or single-breasted jackets!* On three-button jackets, button the top two buttons, a single button at the middle, or just the top one.

The Wandering Waistband

- If you prefer to wear the waistband of your pants low in the front, have them altered at the front to remove length.

- Suspenders will bring the waistline parallel to the floor; never wear suspenders and a belt at the same time.

- Avoid Tight Pants Syndrome[11] because it can cause abdominal discomfort, distension (at times radiating to the chest), heartburn and frequent belching.

Socks

- With professional attire, men should always wear dress socks that are long enough to cover their leg when seated.

- Over-the-calf socks should match your trousers; if that is not possible, match your shoes.

---

[11] Allen, Jane E, "Wardrobe Woes: Hidden Health Hazards of Clothing," ABC News, February 22, 2012, http://abcnews.go.com/Health/wardrobe-woes-hidden-health-hazards-clothing/story?id=15761031&page=2#.UeBUpawbh84

- Avoid brightly coloured and white socks unless you are wearing relaxed business casual attire.

Women's Foundation Garments

- Make sure your lingerie fits well, because not only will it give you the necessary support and help your back, walk and posture, but it will affect the appearance of everything else you wear.
- With semi-transparent tops wear plain skin-toned lingerie. A black, coloured, or patterned bra beneath a white blouse is a definite distraction and image spoiler.
- Periodically have your bra size checked because 80% of women do not wear the correct size.[12]

Jacket Power

- It is particularly important for a woman to wear a jacket because a Canadian study[13] concluded that that a woman wearing a jacket was perceived to have greater expertise and legitimate power than a woman not wearing a jacket.

Skirts and Pants

- Studies show that women who wear skirts or dresses are judged to be more professional and successful than those who wear pants.[14] To have more presence when wearing pants, couple them with a matching jacket, preferably in a dark colour.
- In business, skirts should be no shorter than two to three inches above the knee when standing. Before purchasing a skirt, sit down to check the ease and the length. Avoid skirts that are slit too high or are too tight because not only can they be too revealing and distracting, they'll also limit your movements.

---

[12] "80% of Women Still Wear the Wrong Bra Size!," BeCheeky, November 2010, http://www.prnewswire.com/news-releases/80-of-women-still-wear-the-wrong-bra-size-106595733.html

[13] Temple, Linda E., & Loewen, Karen R., "Perceptions of Power: First Impressions of a Woman Wearing a Jacket." *Perceptual and Motor Skills*, 76, 339-348, 1993.

[14] Davidson, Lynn, "Wear a skirt, not a trouser suit for a better first impression and more success in the workplace," Mail Online, September 19, 2011, http://www.dailymail.co.uk/news/article-2038962/Workplace-gender-inequality-Wear-skirt-trouser-suit-success.html#ixzz1YUxNDa1x

"Busting Out"

- Even when popular culture is in love with cleavage, the necklines of your garments shouldn't be cut too low. If your blouse gapes over your bust due to widely spaced buttons, ask a dressmaker or tailor to sew on an invisible snap at the bust area.

- Make sure that your jackets have adequate room at the bust because if there isn't, the garment will tend to fall away at the front, causing you to continually tug it back to its intended position. Not only is this a nuisance, like cleavage, it draws more attention to your bust instead of your face.

Hosiery

- In spite of a more relaxed attitude regarding women not wearing hosiery to work, when professionally attired, it is an essential accessory. On warm days, choose sheer, nylon microfibers which are cool and almost transparent.

- Neutral hosiery, one or two tones deeper than your skin tone, is always correct. Black, charcoal, grey and navy are also acceptable for business.

- Match the colour of your hose, shoes and hemline to elongate your legs; textured and patterned hose will do the opposite.

- Never wear dark-coloured hose with light shoes; when wearing a trendy coloured hose, match your shoes to your hose.

Handbags

- For business meetings, try to avoid carrying a handbag and portfolio at the same time.

- Your handbag should be in proportion to your height, bone structure and weight, and if you choose a neutral colour, it will coordinate with everything in your wardrobe.

Clothing Maintenance

Taking good care of your clothing will support your image because clean, well-pressed garments look good, no matter what the price.

- To prolong the life of your garments, air them out at the end of the day before storing them in your closet.

- Dampen cotton and linen garments before ironing because steam is never sufficient.

- Use a clothes brush to promptly deal with dried salt, mud, and dirt on the surface of your clothing and an adhesive lint remover will take care of threads and animal hair.
- Check for broken or missing buttons, hems that need repair and signs of wear on collars and cuffs.
- When travelling, never wear a jacket while seated for any length of time because creases will form on the upper arms and back that are very difficult to remove.
- Don't over dry clean your tailored garments because they'll never look as crisp again. Always clean matching pieces together to maintain a uniform colour and if the item is only creased, just have it pressed.

Personal Grooming

Personal grooming is always a sensitive subject, but it can have a great influence on your personal presentation and image. When you take care of your person, others will expect that you are taking care of business.

Hair
- Work with an experienced hair stylist to design a style that flatters your facial features, is up to date, and is suitable for your schedule and your overall image.
- If you colour-enhance your hair, touch it up regularly to avoid unsightly "roots."
- If you have dry scalp, try professional moisturizing products or seek professional help.

Oral Hygiene
- Brush and floss your teeth regularly, especially if you smoke or drink coffee, to avoid bad breath and expensive dental bills. If you use gum to freshen your breath, chew it inconspicuously and then discreetly dispose of it.

Skin Care
- Following a daily skin-care regime to clean your pores, and moisturize your skin will reduce blemishes and leave you with a healthy glow.
- Sun blocks will help you avoid skin discolouration, the dangers associated with excessive sun exposure, and premature aging.

Fingernails

- A good manicure will help you avoid unsightly hangnails. In business settings, don't go to extremes with overly long or flashy nails, and if you bite your fingernails, try to break the habit.

Fragrance

- It is considerate to avoid strong aftershave lotions, perfumes, colognes, deodorants and hair products because they'll invade people's personal space and trigger allergies and asthma.

Smoking Odours

- If you smoke, allow at least 20 minutes from the time you finish your last cigarette to the time you'll be meeting with someone, and use a breath mint.

Shaving

Facial hair on men has been debated for years. A recent study concluded that men with neat, medium-length beards were seen as more trustworthy when selling product, unless the product was underwear.[15] Whatever you do, be consistent.

- If you prefer to be clean shaven, shave daily, and if your skin is sensitive, seek advice from a dermatologist or esthetician.

- If you decide to grow facial hair, keep things neatly trimmed, daily shaving areas that are meant to be clean.

- The style of a moustache, goatee, full or partial beard, etc. should relate to your face shape and the way you want to be perceived.[16] If you are tall with dark hair and pale skin and want to be warm and approachable, adding facial hair may make you seem intimidating.

Makeup

- A small amount of makeup applied to enhance your natural features will go a long way to giving you a more professional image.

---

[15] Bartlett, Tom, "The Trustworthiness of Beards," April 2010, http://chronicle.com/blogs/percolator/the-trustworthiness-of-beards/22581

[16] http://twentytwowords.com/2011/07/25/an-infographic-showing-the-trustworthiness-of-different-styles-of-beards/

- Thirty percent of your facial expression comes from your eyes, so if your eyebrows are not well defined, use an eyebrow pencil or powder to add some definition.

Physical Wellness

You can spend a lot of time, energy and money acquiring an incredible wardrobe. However, if you don't have a healthy diet, aren't physically active and ignore the signs of stress, you may not realize your image potential.

Nutrition

- Your energy level and muscle strength, as well as the colour and texture of your skin, are affected by what you eat and drink, so make good choices, vary your diet, and drink sufficient water.

- If you want to lose weight, consider working with a registered nutritionist to develop an individual dietary plan, and remember that wearing certain clothing can make you appear taller and automatically more slender.

Physical Fitness

- A well-tuned, firm body will enhance your health by boosting your energy, calming anxiety and increasing blood circulation.

- If you find a physical-fitness regime difficult to establish and maintain, use the services of a personal trainer to help you develop a weekly routine that fits your schedule.

Stress and Time Management

- Stress is at the root of many debilitating illnesses and can limit your wealth potential in so many ways. Plan personal time into your schedule and keep abreast of appointments through setting weekly priorities. If you don't manage your stress, it will manage you.

Chapter 5 - At A Glance

Impressions Influence Brand Experiences

First impressions are almost impossible to change. Your appearance is the first thing that people notice when they meet you – often your first calling card – greatly influencing whether they trust you, what they think about you and their overall brand experience.

Dress Strategically for Results

Learn how to strategically use the "ladder of formality" to look powerful or approachable, and then ensure that your wardrobe has a variety of business suits, business casual looks and weekend garments to take you into any context with purpose and confidence.

Details Impact Your Brand Message

A small detail can detract from your brand message. Use the finer details of your clothing, accessories and grooming to continually support your brand and empower your presence, so that others are not distracted from experiencing your true wealth.

Your Platinum Edge: Behaviour

Your behaviour has so much to do with empowering your presence. Why is this? It gives you an opportunity to touch people's lives, build rapport and solidify relationships. If you can accurately read situations, tune into what is considered appropriate and act in thoughtful ways, people will feel comfortable around you. When you treat people with respect and consideration, they'll look for opportunities to spend time with you.

Think back to the people with presence you listed in the exercise in Chapter 1. What principles guide their actions? Are they genuinely interested in you, or do they focus on themselves? Do they affirm you, or do they point out your imperfections? Do they ask for your input, or do they want control of everything? Most likely, they exhibit characteristics that contribute to building relationships rather than destroying them. They might also have a particular confidence and poise, that not only comes with experience, but from purposely making others feel comfortable, which is at the basis of having true wealth and presence.

Good behaviour has a close connection to civility. Civility is not blindly following rigid rules of behaviour in order to appear proper. Although manners play a large role, civility goes much deeper than that. Where there is incivility, you will find rudeness, bullying, and disrespect, all which alienate people. With it comes a cost. Numerous studies in the workplace suggest that incivility reduces productivity, helpfulness, and creativity, and results in the erosion of corporate values and employee loyalty.[1] Also, people who are rude often

---

[1] Pearson, Christine & Porath, Christine, *The Cost of Bad Behavior: How incivility is damaging your business and what to do about it*, Portfolio, Penguin Group, 2009

find that their lives are stalled. They may not realize that they show rudeness because it's very difficult for people to recognize it in themselves. If they do become aware of it and change their actions, they will undoubtedly see new relationships flourish over time.

So what exactly is civility? Dr. P. M. Forni, professor at Johns Hopkins University, co-founder of the Johns Hopkins Civility Project and widely respected civility expert says it is, "a code of behaviour based on respect, restraint and responsibility."[2] You might immediately think about saying "please" or "thank you;" not talking with your mouth full; giving your seat on a bus to person with a disability; opening doors for elderly people; maintaining confidentialities; not lying on your resume; and many other things.

All these do show signs of civility; however, there is more to civility than the actions themselves. When you look at the literal meaning of the word which comes from the Latin *civitas* meaning "city," in the sense of community, you're also recognizing that it involves people and the good of society as a whole. It isn't about using the right fork, but eating in a way that makes others feel comfortable. If the paper in the photocopier is low when you finish using it, do you fill it, regardless of your position? When a client needs to see you after business hours, do you set aside your plans to accommodate this person? "We are civil when we believe that other people's claim to comfort and happiness is as valid as our own, and we back up belief with action (such as letting someone merge into the flow of traffic)," says Dr. Forni.[3]

When you have a genuine interest in other people and act towards them in ways that show civility, regardless of their status or your agenda, you create harmony and community and along the way, empower your presence.

Etiquette and Manners

How do etiquette and manners relate to civility? They involve showing respect, restraint and responsibility towards others, which will positively impact relationships. But are etiquette and manners the same? Etiquette is associated with knowing and strictly following rules of social behaviour. Many of

---

[2] Forni, P.M., *Choosing Civility: The Twenty-five Rules of Considerate Conduct*, St. Martin's Griffin, 2002

[3] Forni, P.M., "The Other Side of Civility," May 26, 2009, http://krieger.jhu.edu/civility/ArticlesandPressReleases.html

the rules were adopted for very logical reasons which still hold true today, while others have evolved over centuries. For example, replying in a timely manner to an invitation with a R.S.V.P., which is an acronym for the French phrase, *Répondez s'il vous plait* (Please reply), continues to be appreciated by hosts who need to prepare refreshments. Having good manners transcends the rigidity of etiquette because it has to do with always showing consideration for others and their welfare, like waiting to enter an office until the person inside is off the phone, keeping your voice down in public places, or never gossiping.

At times you might even break a rule of etiquette to show good manners. For instance at a very formal reception, it is the host's responsibility to propose the first toast to the guest of honour. If an eager guest who is unaware of this tradition proposes this toast, the host shouldn't appear inconvenienced, but instead enthusiastically raise a glass along with everyone else. As you can see, etiquette is about using the right fork, but having manners involves eating in a way that makes others feel comfortable, regardless of which fork you use.

When all else is equal, using good etiquette and manners will set you apart from others. That being said, knowing the finer points of etiquette will put you at ease in any situation, regardless of your socio-economic background, adding to your presence. When you are free from worry about how to make a proper introduction, handle a dining dilemma, work a room like a pro, or act appropriately in some other environment, you'll be able to genuinely focus on the well-being of the people that you are with, enriching their experiences.

Be Responsible at Work

Your reputation as a reliable person is essential to your success in the workplace. Keep appointments and promises, and never promise what you can't deliver because that will erode trust. There should be no surprises for your clients regarding your products or services. If you are using associates or subcontractors to complete work, you are answerable for their behaviour; make sure that they understand their responsibilities and keep things under control.

Manage Your Time: Chronic lateness dramatically influences the way you and your organization are perceived by existing and potential customers. Show your responsibility by prioritizing your commitments, setting realistic timelines (including travel time), and building in buffers for unexpected situations.

Handle Interruptions: Be prepared for interruptions, and discipline yourself to quickly refocus your energies once a problem is resolved. If a colleague arrives unannounced and you have a deadline to meet, politely ask the person to return at a scheduled time. If a customer needs your attention and the situation isn't urgent, suggest, "You deserve my undivided attention, so I'd like to schedule an appointment with you for tomorrow to take care of this before the due date."

Show Respect across Generations: Defend colleagues when they've been wronged, and when it's necessary to correct someone, do it privately. Treating everyone with respect, whatever their age, status or corporate agenda will create a healthy and productive work environment. Often a person further down the chain of command can provide valuable insight, so you want to keep all lines of communication open. This will be explained further in Chapter 8 which looks into multi-generational approaches to empowering presence.

Electronic Devices: Electronic devices have the power to immediately connect you with anyone in the world, but they also have the power to destroy communication just as quickly. They are a natural part of our work day, but because they are so present, care must be taken not to use them at times when you want to build relationships with someone you are with. Even using your cell phone to check the time can be misinterpreted as disinterest.

Respecting Territory: Don't invade people's personal space by barging into their office, speaking too loudly (especially in an open office), or standing too close to them. Also, when you touch objects in other people's offices or sit on their desks, they'll see you as domineering and intimidating.[4]

Loyalty Inside and Out: A disgruntled employee can create a destructive atmosphere at work, but an organization's reputation can also be damaged if this person is negative in the community. Be positive and supportive towards staff at all times in order to foster communication. Staff should be encouraged to discuss concerns with management because there may be an acceptable explanation for something that on the surface appears unfair.

---

[4] Bowden, Mark, *Winning Body Language: Control the Conversation, Command Attention, and Convey the Right Message without Saying a Word*, McGraw Hill, 2010

Be Generous: A generous spirit will open many doors of opportunity. Take time to congratulate colleagues, acknowledge favours, and give credit where credit is due. Don't hoard information, but rather keep people abreast of things; ultimately it is more productive.

Giving and Receiving Gifts: If an organization has a "no gift" policy, it needs to be communicated to staff and suppliers to avoid awkward situations. If you're doing business in the global marketplace, research their customs so that you act appropriately. For example, giving a clock to someone in China would not be positive because it is associated with death. Likewise, in Japan where giving gifts in business is common, the gift exchanged can be quite simple, but the ceremony involved in giving it will usually be elaborate.[5]

Apologizing: It takes character to admit you're wrong. Apologizing shows good business sense because unresolved conflicts result in bitterness, destroying relationships. Also, clients are more loyal to firms that apologize than to those who have no problems. Apologies should be honest, straightforward and sincere, with no attempt to justify your actions.

Shaking Hands

Establishing rapport with people is essential when building trust and a handshake is the quickest, most effective way to do it. If you knew that you'd have to spend three hours interacting with a person to get the same connection that one handshake could get you, you'd never forgo shaking hands again.[6] A handshake will tell you a lot about the person that you are meeting, and he or she will also use the opportunity to form opinions about you. Have you ever thought about what your handshake says? Ponder this as you review these tips on shaking hands:

- Always stand to shake hands if you are able to do so. Smile, make eye contact and extend your right arm towards the other person with your hand in a vertical position with the thumb on top; grasp the other person's whole hand firmly so that the webs between your thumbs and first fingers

[5] Morrison, Terri & Conaway, Wayne A., *Kiss, Bow, Or Shake Hands: The Bestselling Guide to Doing Business in More Than 60 Countries*, Adams Media Corporation, 1995, 2006, Terri Morrison

[6] Wood, Patti, "The Secret of the Perfect Handshake," 2007, http://www.pattiwood.net/article.asp?PageID=2490

and your palms touch. Shake two to five times, and then release. If you want to increase the other person's status, slightly rotate your hand in a clockwise direction, giving them the upper hand.[7]

- If you need to shake with your left hand, simply twist your wrist in a clockwise direction until you can fully grasp the other person's right hand. If you encounter someone who has no hands, resist to the urge to react nervously. The person may extend an elbow, shoulder or foot, so shake whatever is offered with your usual warmth, and without comment.

- In business, gender does not influence handshakes, so don't hesitate to extend your hand or the person you are meeting may think that you're inexperienced. The only exception is when physical contact with the opposite gender isn't culturally acceptable.

- If your hands sweat, place a handkerchief sprayed with an unscented antiperspirant into your right pocket and inconspicuously wipe your hand on it before extending your hand.

- If you're at an event where cold drinks are being served, hold your glass in your left hand.

Handshakes to Avoid

The Bone Crusher: Avoid crushing the other person's hand by waiting a split second before bearing down and then match their firmness. This is especially important if someone has arthritis or some other condition.

The Cold Fish: A tentative, limp handshake will leave others feeling as if they've touched a day-old mackerel. They'll question your authority and confidence. In some cultures, however, gentle handshakes are the norm.

The Two-Handed Clasp: Cupping another person's hand in both of yours during a handshake should be reserved for close friends and family members.

The Touchy-Feely: In business, putting your left hand on the other person's arm, shoulder or back while shaking hands is too familiar.

The Upper Hand: Twisting your hand counter-clockwise to achieve an upper-handed position establishes your superiority, but it can be seen as domineering.

---

[7] Bowden, Mark, *Winning Body Language: Control the Conversation, Command Attention, and Convey the Right Message – Without Saying a Word*, McGraw Hill, 2010

Introductions

Knowing how to introduce friends and colleagues makes social and business situations easier and certainly increases your poise and presence. We've all encountered awkward circumstances when people fail to introduce us to those whom they know, so that we are left to our own devices. This is not only rude, but it also creates a real communication barrier because it is more difficult to enter into conversation with them. Sometimes it's because people are uncertain as to how to make introductions, so they avoid them. At other times, they forgo them because they've forgotten the other person's name. If this happens to you, simply say, "I'm so sorry. Your name has just slipped my mind. Please remind me of it," and then continue on with an enthusiastic introduction. If you sense that someone is struggling to recall your name, come to their rescue by shaking the other person's hand and introduce yourself.

There are many factors involved in making proper introductions. One thing is certain: it's better to attempt an introduction than to worry about semantics. If you make a mistake, most people won't notice. Here are the basic guidelines:

- Introduce the younger or less honoured person to the older or more honoured person.

- The older person, the one who has the higher rank, the "guest" (someone entering the circle), and a woman (in a social context) are most honoured.

- Always say the name of the older or more honoured person first.

- In formal situations or where there is a great age difference use titles such as "Mr." or "Ms."

- Give the people you are introducing some information about each other so they will immediately have something to talk about. For example, "George Brodeur, I want you to meet Kim Bennett who is a journalism student. By the way, George is a talented writer..."

> Standard introduction: "Ms. Black (older/more honoured),
> I'd like you to meet John Smith (younger/less honoured)."

Notice in this example, I've used "meet" instead of "introduce" because invariably people will say: "Ms. Black, I'd like to introduce you to John Smith." By using the preposition "to" twice, suddenly the tables are turned, making John more important than Ms. Black. When you use the word introduce, this is correct: "Ms. Black, I'd like to introduce John Smith." In informal situations, "Deborah, this is John," would suffice.

If you do commit an obvious social blunder while introducing someone, don't panic! Graceful spontaneity will come to the rescue when good manners prevail. Say that you are sorry, and then begin the introduction again.

Telephone Etiquette

Your initial contact with people is often over the phone, so the way that you answer it will set the mood for the conversation. The following points will help you make a prime impression.

- Always smile when you answer the telephone, because it will make you sound approachable and friendly, and use a clear articulate voice.
- If you're feeling rushed, take a deep breath before you answer the telephone.
- Have patience with those who need more time to explain the purpose of their call. In our fast-paced society, it's easy to be abrupt in an attempt to move the conversation along.
- If you are with someone when the phone rings, let the call go to voicemail.
- Don't answer your cell phone in a public area such as a theatre, restaurant, lecture hall or place of worship; your conversation will interrupt other's enjoyment of the space.
- When making calls, let the telephone ring six to ten times because not everyone can answer a phone in three rings.
- Return calls within 24 hours, even if you don't yet have an answer to their question.
- To prevent time-consuming telephone tag, when leaving a message, clearly give your contact information and reason for calling, so that the person may also leave you a detailed message if they encounter your voicemail.
- Don't take your calls in areas with annoying background noise. While talking on the telephone, don't speak to another person in the room, eat, smoke, drink or tap on your keyboard.

Meeting Etiquette

You reveal a lot about yourself and your potential in a meeting. It's the perfect arena for demonstrating your leadership, social acumen, communication style, and presentation skills. Most people dislike attending meetings because they're often disorganized, too little gets accomplished and time has been wasted. Only call a meeting when you have a clear purpose, because if you can't articulate it, how can you expect the participants to fully contribute? Consider whether you can achieve just as much via teleconference, e-mail or virtual means. If you've decided that face-to-face interaction is best, these guidelines will help you effectively manage your meetings:

Timing Considerations

- Avoid calling a meeting when people are tired or preoccupied, such as at the end of a day or just before a long weekend.
- Give proper advanced notice so the participants can block off time in their schedules.
- Start meetings on time, even if everyone hasn't arrived, to show respect to those who were prompt.

Who Should Attend?

- Invite open-minded people who are not afraid to express their ideas.
- Only those who are directly involved should be present because it is easier to make decisions with smaller groups.

The Agenda

- Draw up a concise agenda stating the meeting purpose, location, items to be discussed, time allocations, and the person responsible for each item to be discussed so that everyone knows what to expect and can prepare.

Seating

- At a rectangular table, the Chair usually sits at one end, and senior management and honoured guests sit on either side.
- If participants' seating isn't assigned, to build presence, choose a spot where you'll be noticed by the decision makers.
- If you need to mitigate a confrontation, avoid sitting directly opposite the person in question in order to have the least amount of eye contact as possible.

The Role of the Chair

- Ensure that the essential people are present. Welcome participants and introduce those who don't know each other.
- Lay down the ground rules, conduct the meeting according to the agenda, and keep discussions on track, always encouraging everyone to fully participate and show respect to one another.

The Role of the Participant

- Arrive on time with your homework done and introduce yourself to those you don't know.
- Turn off your cell phone and behave in a professional way: sit upright, appear alert, don't play with objects on the table, and actively listen.
- If you need to leave the meeting for a moment, politely excuse yourself and re-enter quietly.
- Speaking up early in the meeting will assert your presence, as long as you are familiar with the topic being discussed and have something valuable to add.
- Don't be afraid to ask intelligent, clarifying questions.
- If you're not being listened to, politely ask for a response with: "Before we discuss fundraising, I'd appreciate hearing the group's response to what I've said."
- When you propose a new idea or solution, use tact but don't undermine yourself. "I don't know if this will work" isn't as effective as "There is a possible solution here. Has this ever been tried…?"

Additional Points for Teleconferences

- When you join the call, announce yourself. Once most people are on the line, the Chair will verify who is present and call the meeting to order, following the agenda and timeline closely.
- Only one person should talk at a time; state your name before you speak each time because not everyone will know your voice.
- Don't create background noise by breathing heavily into the phone, rustling paper, keyboarding, etc. Use a mute button when possible.

Handling Meeting Challenges

There will always be challenges in meetings that try the patience of everyone. To maintain your professional stance, it's important to handle these situations with tact so that no one loses face and the meeting isn't disrupted.

Late Arrivals: When someone comes in late, don't repeat the material that has already been covered because it wastes time and penalizes those who arrived promptly.

Reluctant Participants: To encourage people who are hesitant to speak up, instead of saying: "You haven't said anything during the whole meeting," try: "I know you've worked on this project, and we'd value your opinion. Perhaps you can give this some thought and I'll come back to you later in the meeting."

Constant Commentators: Thank people who continually express their opinions for their contributions and then immediately ask to hear from others. In addition, at the beginning of the meeting, you could lay some ground rules that include holding comments until everything has been presented, or break the participants into groups for discussion and have them report back.

Private Conversations: So as not to confront people who talk to their neighbours during a meeting with equal rudeness, tactfully invite them to share their comments with the whole group, or just be silent and wait for their talking to cease.

Highjackers: When a participant tries to lead the discussion away from the planned agenda to their pet projects, the Chair can place the item in the "Issue Bin" until the end of the meeting, when other business is covered, time permitting.

Put-Downs: To handle people who believe that their ideas are the only ones worth considering, the Chair can remind the whole group that personal experiences may differ and that all views are valid, even if they're unusual or unpopular.

When meetings are over and work takes you outside the office, there are many occasions to encounter new people. Most individuals are not intimidated when speaking one-on-one with someone they don't know; however, when they have to enter a room of strangers, it becomes a different story. When I've asked people if they love going into a room of strangers and striking up conversations, only 4% of them, including the most educated and experienced business professionals, said that they did, while the rest had varying degrees of discomfort. I've found only one notable exception. About 40% of seasoned financial advisors and insurance agents answered in the affirmative. Most likely it is because this activity provides them with perfect opportunities for them to build their businesses, and as with any skill, it becomes easier with practice.

How to Work a Room with Ease

Business mixers, cocktail hours, networking events, and informal receptions are occasions that give you a chance to meet new people, and keep in touch with friends, colleagues and clients. People with presence seem to navigate the room with such ease, stopping to talk with others for just the right amount of time before moving on. Although you may doubt it, everyone can learn techniques to make the process easier. If the thought of entering a room full of strangers sends chills up your spine, the following ten strategies will help you develop new techniques so that you can look forward to such gatherings with more confidence than you have now.

1. Accept That Nervousness Is Natural
- At a young age, your parents taught you not to talk to strangers, so entering a room filled with them is naturally uncomfortable.
- To reduce anxiety, it is important to first acknowledge your fear, and then redefine the "strangers" you're about to meet by finding some common ground. At a business mixer, you can assume that everyone is interested in business. At a fundraiser, you are all supporting a cause. At a wedding, everyone knows the bride or the groom. Armed with this knowledge, the people you're about to meet are not so "strange" after all.

2. Plan Your Clothing
- As discussed in Chapter 5, dress appropriately with a strategy in mind and if the dress is business casual, be careful not to bottom out.
- Choose garments that have pockets for your business cards if possible, so that you can leave purses and portfolios at home.

3. Be Prepared
- Set a goal to meet two to three new people so that you don't congregate with those you already know. Bring a good supply of business cards.

- Come prepared to talk about three to five timely topics. Positive current events, human-interest stories, sports, theatre and movies are far more interesting than the weather.
- Use positive self-talk because studies show that it affects outcomes.[8] Replace, "I don't like meeting people; I'd rather be home watching TV," with, "I know I'm going to meet some incredible people this evening, and enjoy our conversations."

4. Make a Deliberate Entrance

- Don't slink into the room and cower in a corner.
- A confident, upright posture actually helps to quiet your nerves[9], so with your head held high, walk with a sense of purpose at least a quarter of the way into the room, take a few unflustered seconds to survey the group, and then follow your instincts about whom to approach.

5. Handling Drinks and Hors D'oeuvres

- Eat before the event so that people are your main focus, and drink responsibly.
- Here's how to hold a napkin, plate and glass all in your left hand so that you can still shake hands:
  1) Place the stem of a wine glass through your baby finger and ring finger and use the tips of those two fingers and the muscle of your thumb to hold the bowl of the glass securely.
  2) Straighten your middle finger and pointer finger and place your napkin between them.
  3) Balance the plate on the straightened pointer finger, keeping it level by using your thumb to put pressure on the edge of the plate.
- Take only one or two pieces of food at a time, spoon dipping sauces onto your plate, use your napkin liberally to wipe your fingers and carefully dispose of toothpicks. Beware of hot hors d'oeuvres that could burn your mouth, *bruschetta* that could tumble down your shirt, and phyllo pastry

---

[8] Campbell, Polly, "Positive self talk can help you win the race--or the day," June 2011, http://www.psychologytoday.com/blog/imperfect-spirituality/201106/positive-self-talk-can-help-you-win-the-race-or-the-day

[9] Bowden, Mark, *Winning Body Language: Control the Conversation, Command Attention, and Convey the Right Message without Saying a Word*, McGraw Hill, 2010

that has a tendency to coat your lips. Sometimes it is better not to eat at all!

6. Avoid Approaching Two People

- Avoid the tendency to gravitate to people you already know and don't approach two people on their own because you may be interrupting a private conversation.

- A person who is alone will usually be relieved if you walk up to them, or choose a group of three or more people who seem to be having fun and are in an open circle where there is a space that you can fill. If you make eye contact with one of them, typically they'll bring you into the group.

7. Break the Ice

- Don't wait for a proper introduction. Break the ice with a friendly "hello," extend your hand and give a firm handshake, and introduce yourself with your seven-second self-introduction or personal brand statement that you developed in Chapter 3.

- Behave like a host by introducing people you encounter to others. If they are not comfortable with working a room, they will be forever grateful and you will be remembered.

8. Master Small Talk

- Concentrate on asking others about themselves and use the topics you prepared before the event.

- Avoid sensitive subjects, listen more than you speak and ask open-ended questions. A skilled conversationalist will always manage to realign the focus in their direction when they need to.

- You will find a 5-step small talk sequence that you can use, concluding with how to graciously break away in Chapter 7.

9. Focus on Contacts, Not Contracts

- Your goal should be to make meaningful contacts, not close deals in the short time that a cocktail party or mixer affords.

- If you think that the person you're talking to can help you, or if you believe that you have valuable contacts for them, ask if you can continue the conversation at another time.

- Exchange contact information electronically or give each other a business card.

10. Follow Up Effectively

- Review your goals and if you didn't meet three to five new people, plan to try something different the next time.

- If you promised to give someone information or you asked to meet with them again, follow through and arrange to have coffee or lunch. A telephone call will be more personal than an email and it will give you an added opportunity to assess their level of interest.

If your invitation to have a meal with a contact has been accepted, you need to ensure that things run smoothly. For details on how to properly host a business lunch, please refer to Chapter 9. Also as the host, your guest will be following your lead. If you have a good understanding of dining etiquette, you'll be able to relax and concentrate on getting to know the other person.

Dining Etiquette Basics

All of our senses are involved with dining, which makes time spent at the table very memorable. Having a meal with someone gives you an uninterrupted opportunity to get to know each other, which is essential for creating trust and rapport. However, for some people, this is an anxious time. A large number of adults admit to not knowing which fork to use or where their bread plate is located. It's not surprising because with busy schedules and eating on the run, dining etiquette is rarely taught in homes today.

Having a firm grasp of dining protocol is essential because futures can be decided over meals. There is something about the dining table that makes it a proving ground for prospective employees, candidates for promotion, and potential suppliers. A sales manager even told me that he timed interviewees while they looked at the menu. If they took more than one minute to decide what to order, he wouldn't hire them because he needed people who could be decisive. Others say that people who salt their food before tasting it are rash decision makers. You never know what people might be thinking.

Knowing dining protocol is an essential image management skill for any serious business professional. Your polite behaviour at the table will signal a certain sensitivity and leadership potential that people will remember. If you freeze at the beginning of a meal, waiting for someone else to make the first move because you're not sure where your bread plate is located, wouldn't you like to have peace of mind about this? The following guidelines are appropriate in formal dining environments. If you know what to do there, you'll be confident in all situations, including ones where the cutlery is rolled into a paper napkin.

Seating and Personal Objects

- If you're the host, ensure that your guest has the best seat in the restaurant – whether it is the nicest view, or the quietest location.

- Personal items such as keys, glasses, and cell phones are not placed on the table. If they won't fit in your pockets, bring a purse, tote or portfolio with you, and depending on its size, place it on your lap, the back of the chair or out of the way on the floor.

Table Setting

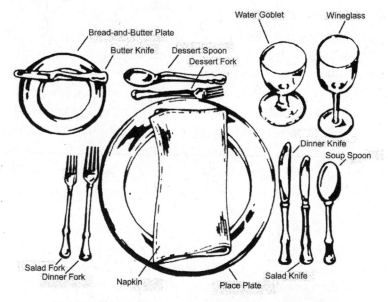

A table setting for a four-course meal that includes soup, salad, main course, rolls, and dessert

- The number of pieces of flatware is determined by the menu and the formality of the meal.

- Flatware is placed nearest the hand that will be holding it when eating Continental style. Forks, with the exception of a seafood fork, will be on the left and knives and spoons on the right.

- Utensils that are on the outside will be used first, with the inner flatware being reserved for subsequent courses. When in doubt, follow your host. If there is no host assigned, keep your eye on someone at the table who appears confident; be prepared to lead if you are the host.

Where is Your Bread Plate?

- It is located to the left of your fork(s), and your water glass is above your dinner knife on the right. You can always remember this by using one of these two methods:

  A) With your hands just above your lap, bring the tips of your pointer fingers and thumbs together to form a circle with each hand. Straighten your other fingers and rotate your hands so that the circles are uppermost. You will notice that your left hand forms a "b" for "bread" and the right one, a "d" for "drink."

  B) If you like BMWs, you use this acronym: bread, meal, and water. English is read from the left to right, so the bread plate is on the left, the meal in the middle, and your water glass on the right.

Handling Cups, Glasses and Wine

- Coffee mugs and tea cups are picked up by the handles. Don't elevate your little finger in an affected manner, nor place your entire hand around the cup. Leave cups and mugs on the table when being served.

- Short-stemmed water glasses are held at the base of the bowl with your thumb and first two fingers. Pick up tumblers near the base.

- Long-stemmed wine glasses and champagne flutes are held by the stem just beneath the bowl to maintain the temperature of the contents and to avoid fingerprints on the bowl. If you don't wish to have wine, don't turn your glass upside down or place your hand firmly over the opening. Instead politely say to the wait staff, "No, thank you."

Napkin Nuances

- At a hosted dinner party, wait until the host places the napkin on his or her lap before you do, otherwise put it on your lap as soon as you sit down. Fold your napkin in half and place it with the crease towards you.

- Never tuck your napkin into your belt, shirt or collar. Some specialty napkins have a buttonhole on one corner; resist the urge to attach it to your shirt.

- If you need to be excused from the table during the meal, pick up your folded napkin and fold it so that the soiled area is concealed, and place it on the left between your dinner and bread plates. Some etiquette experts will also suggest that you place it on the chair, but you run the risk of soiling the upholstery or picking up germs.
- When you've finished your meal, loosely fold your napkin and place it either to the left of your dessert plate, or if it's been removed, in the middle of your place setting.

When Do You Begin Eating?

Dinner party: When the host is served and picks up his or her fork to begin, or when the host encourages you to start. This also avoids the embarrassing situation where you begin to eat and then the host asks for a moment to give thanks for the food.

Round table: When everyone's food has been served.

Buffet: When you've served yourself some food, and one other person joins you at the dining table.

Table Conduct

- If a utensil appears soiled, don't wipe it on your napkin. Politely ask for a clean one.
- Sit up straight at the table and keep your elbows close to your body, even when cutting your food. For each bite, lean forward slightly by pivoting from the waist (still with a straight back), and bring the food up to your mouth, not your mouth down to your food. Never lick your knife.
- Once a utensil is used, it should remain fully on your plate, never touching the table again.
- Place only your wrists on the table when pausing and never punctuate your conversation by stabbing the air with your utensils.
- Take modest bites so that your face isn't distorted, eat quietly with your mouth closed, and don't talk with your mouth full. Pace yourself to finish your meal at about the same time as your dining companion(s).
- Pick up items only if they are within easy reach or ask for them to be passed to you.

- If you need to leave the table during the meal to go to the washroom, if possible, wait for an appropriate time such as between courses, and then excuse yourself and return quickly. Do not leave the table to have a cigarette, make a phone call or speak to someone else in the dining room.

Passing and Adding

- Food is usually passed to the right; always pass the salt and pepper as a pair.
- Don't serve yourself community food (sugar, salt, pepper, salad dressing, bread, etc.) until you first offer it to someone else.
- Don't add salt and pepper or sauces to food before tasting it. In a fine restaurant or in someone's home, it's rude to ask for condiments if they are not on the table.

Handling Utensils

There are certain recommended ways to hold and use your utensils when cutting and eating food. While the following guidelines are written for people who are right-handed, people who eat with their left hand can reverse the directions.

When eating with one utensil:

- Never grasp the handle of a utensil with a fist or use the side of your fork to cut something.
- Hold the utensil like a pen, grasping the fork or spoon with your thumb and forefinger about three-quarters of the way up the handle. Your other three fingers are underneath, with the weight of the utensil resting on your middle finger. Press your thumb down from the top for added security.

When cutting food with two utensils:

- Never hold the fork perpendicular to the plate in a fist-like death grip and saw back and forth with your knife. Cut one piece and eat it before cutting another.
- Place your knife diagonally across your right hand with the end of the handle at the crease where your smallest finger joins your hand, and the area where the handle meets the blade at the tip of your pointer finger. Wrap the rest of your fingers and thumb around the handle, then turn

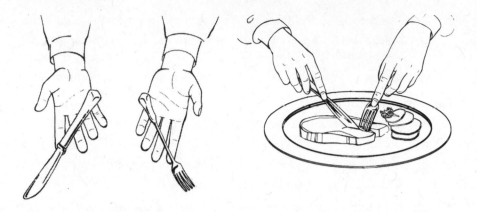

your hand over so the blade is vertical and your pointer finger is on top, ready to press down when cutting.

- Place the fork with the tines up across your open left hand in the same manner as the knife, with the end of the handle at the crease where your smallest finger joins your hand and the area where the fork widens out at the tip of your pointer finger. Grasp the handle and turn your hand over so that the tines of the fork are down. To maintain good control, keep your first finger tip on the back of the fork just above where the fork widens.

- The ends of the handles of both utensils should be hidden inside your hands when cutting and eating using the Continental style.

Eating Styles

- There are two general ways of handling your utensils: the American and the Continental. Both styles are acceptable in North America, with the Continental style being the preferred mode in formal, upper-class settings, usually in Britain. Many Europeans find the Continental style stuffy and use a less rigid approach of their own.

- Food is cut the same way with both styles. It is how you convey the food to your fork and mouth that differ. Use the style that is most comfortable and practical for the type of food you're eating and the company you are with.

American Style

With American style, after cutting a piece of food, the knife is put down across the upper right edge of the dinner plate with the sharp edge towards you, and the fork is transferred to the right hand with tines up and is used to transfer the food to your mouth.

Continental Style

With the Continental style, the entire meal is eaten with the knife in the right hand and the fork in the left hand (with tines down). Once a morsel is cut, it is either pierced with the fork or the knife is used to push it onto the back of · the fork. Then with the fork still in the left hand with the tines down, the food is transferred to the mouth.

Flatware Semaphore

It's important to realize that how you position your utensils gives signals to the wait staff.

Pausing Position

Rest both utensils across your plate in an inverted 'V' position. Place your knife so that the handle is at the lower right of your plate and the tip of the blade is near the centre with the cutting edge turned inward, in a non-confrontational way. Place your fork with tines down in the equivalent position but with the handle at the lower left of your plate.

Finished Position

When you're finished your meal, place your knife on the right of your plate as if you are pausing. Place your fork below and parallel to the knife, with the tines up if you're eating American style, or down with the Continental style.

Rolls and Bread

When there's no host to get the basket of rolls moving, and it is within easy reach, pick it up, open the linen cover, hold onto the basket firmly and offer it to the person on your left. Then choose a roll yourself, place it on your bread plate and hold the basket so that the person on your right can also take a roll, and put it on their bread plate. This person then takes the basket from you and offers a roll to the one on their right, and so on. Should the first person take the basket from your hands, let it proceed to the left.

- When butter is passed to you, use the serving utensil provided to move a small amount of butter onto your bread plate and return the utensil to the butter plate before you pass it on.

- Never move your bread plate to the middle of your table setting while you wait for your main course to arrive, and make sure all the activity surrounding the buttering of your roll or bread happens over the bread plate.

- How you butter your roll will tell others a lot about you. Don't cut or tear a roll in half and butter the whole thing. Instead, pull off a bite-sized piece, use your own butter spreader located on your bread plate to place a small amount of butter on it, and then place the spreader down across the bread plate, and eat the morsel. If no butter spreader is provided, use your dinner knife and when it is not in use, place it fully on the bread plate until your dinner arrives.

- When bread is served, take one slice at a time and either handle it as you would a roll, eating it piece by piece, or break the slice of bread in half and butter each half just before you eat it.

Soup

- Spoon soup away from you and don't blow on hot soup. Instead, make conversation with your dining partner until it has cooled enough.

- When eating soup, hold the side of the spoon parallel to your lips and tip the liquid into your mouth without slurping. Cream soups are best eaten with a smaller round cream soup spoon that fits easily into your mouth.

- Don't dunk your roll or drop crushed crackers into your soup.

- To finish your soup, tip the bowl away from you and spoon one or two times.

- When pausing or finished, place your spoon on the plate beneath the soup bowl.

Salad

- Cut crisp, unmanageable pieces of lettuce with your fork and knife; for more pliable pieces, use your utensils to fold them several times to make small packets.

- If you find a bug in your salad, quietly ask for the wait staff to remove your plate. In formal settings, stop eating and don't mention it to the others at the table because it would make them uncomfortable and embarrass the host.

Dealing with Dinnertime Dilemmas

- If food gets caught in your teeth, don't pick at it. Instead, drink water to try to dislodge the offending morsel, or go to the washroom to remove it.

- If you spill something on the table in a restaurant, apologize to your dining partners and ask the wait staff for assistance. If you spill something on the table in someone's home, apologize and offer to help clean it up.

- If you lose control of a utensil and it falls to the tablecloth, apologize, pick it up and continue eating. If it falls to the floor, ask the wait staff for another one.

- If you encounter gristle, bones or inedible bits while you're eating, don't spit them into your napkin. Bring your fork to your mouth, use your tongue to push the offending morsel onto your fork, and then put it onto your dinner plate (not your bread plate).

- If an olive goes into your mouth using your fingers (as it might if you took one from an appetizer dish), use your fingers to remove the pit and place it on the bread plate. If it entered your mouth on a fork, for example when eating a Greek salad, the pit should be removed with your fork and be placed out of the way on the salad plate, rather than the bread plate.

- If a piece of food falls onto the table, apologize to your dining partner, pick it up and place it off to one side on your plate.

- When squeezing fresh lemon on your food, pick up the lemon wedge, push the tines of your fork into the middle of the cut side and squeeze the ends together. The fork ensures that the lemon doesn't slip out of your fingers, and it helps direct the flow of the juice toward your food.

- If you've placed extremely hot soup or food into your mouth, don't spit it out. Quickly take a sip of cold water to cool your palate.

- Dessert can be eaten with a spoon or fork, depending upon what is served. If you have something difficult to eat, such as a poached pear on a meringue, use a spoon in your right hand to steady the item and a fork in the left hand to break off a bite-sized piece and push it onto the spoon.

- Just as it is impolite to comb your hair at the table, don't apply lip balm or lipstick, or touch up your makeup at the table.
- When eating breakfast at a networking event, be careful not to bring certain habits you may have into the public eye, such as smashing the yolks of your eggs and using a piece of toast in your hand to sop them up, using your fingers to push the last bit of your scrambled eggs onto your fork, or eating limp bacon by dangling it in the air until your mouth is positioned under one end.

Showing Your Appreciation

In the hectic pace of life, saying "thank you" has almost become a dying art. Acknowledging staff and colleagues for a job well done is an effective way to encourage excellence. A note of thanks sent within a reasonable amount of time for a gift you've received, a special dinner, a testimonial, a business referral, etc. will enhance your image and your relationships. The format you use will depend on the context.

Typed Letter: Use it to thank firms for their time and business. Also research shows that 82% of executives say that candidates should send a follow up thank-you letter after an interview to let the employer know you are interested in the job and really enjoyed meeting with them.[10]

Handwritten Note: Use it when you want to be more personal in a business setting. It's also good for showing appreciation for special social engagements, such as holding a dinner in your honour. Sending handwritten thank-you notes to your clients will definitely be remembered as it is seldom done.

Electronic Message: Use it to thank someone you know well for a business lunch, a referral, or other acts of kindness and consideration.

Telephone Call: This can be used in place of all the above expressions of thanks. As well, it provides you with the best opportunity to connect on a more personal level, giving you another opportunity to touch someone in a memorable way.

---

[10] "Five Reasons You Don't Have a Job," Healthy Investment – Improved Profit, July 2013, http://w.hiip.ca/?p=683

Chapter 6 - At A Glance

Show Respect, Restraint & Responsibility

In all your interactions, you have a choice to show congeniality and build relationships. If you act with respect, restraint and responsibility, always giving other people deference, you will demonstrate true civility. A follow-up to the "first impressions" of appearance, this is the foundation for meaningful interactions which, over time, certainly consolidates and empowers your presence.

Etiquette and Manners Increase Presence

Knowing the etiquette and manners for all social and business situations will make you unflappable, no matter what the circumstances, enabling you to relax and fully focus on people around you, enriching their experiences. If things don't seem to work out the "proper" way, have the freedom to laugh at yourself, so that you can continue on with confidence.

Civility is Transformative

A moment of kindness – a thoughtful deed – can be a transforming experience for you the giver, as well as for everyone else. "Paying it forward," reciprocating kindness and acknowledging the good in others, will truly empower your presence and add richness to their lives, too.

Your Platinum Edge: Communication

Communication is involved in all human connection. In fact, almost nothing happens in life without some form of it, whether verbal, written or nonverbal. Even if you refuse to communicate with someone, it doesn't stop the process, because you are still sending the person a message. The other person will be forced to think about your inaction and may wonder if you are displeased, disorganized or truly unprofessional. Obviously, it is better to communicate clearly with someone rather than leaving things to such anxious speculation.

Poor communication is costly. A vague email addressing a simple matter that requires a whirlwind of messages to clarify a request takes valuable time away from other priorities. An awkward, indecisive conversation with a client could put future business in jeopardy. Inattentive body language during a meeting could ruin the possibilities of a promotion. The inability to put good ideas into words could hinder future prospects in any endeavour.

When there is good communication, there are fewer misunderstandings and disagreements, and the sense of community that is associated with true civility, is enhanced. People with good communication skills have the ability to create trust, good morale, and respect with colleagues, clients, suppliers, family members, and everyone else in their lives. They're also able to deliver difficult information with sensitivity and handle customer concerns with tact, avoiding conflict and broken relationships.

Research has been done for decades, regarding the skills that companies look for in potential employees, and "good communication" is consistently at the top of the list. Team building is second, which also requires leaders and members to communicate well. When people are able to readily contribute their expertise while respecting the opinions of others, discussions are fruitful, risk is mitigated and problems are solved.

According to an article in the *Harvard Business Review*,[1] climbing the corporate ladder is directly related to strong communication skills. The presence necessary to carry responsibilities at that level partly have to do with having the right image, but dress and grooming alone are not enough. Executive presence "ultimately boils down to your ability to project mature self-confidence, a sense that you can take control of difficult, unpredictable situations; make tough decisions in a timely way and hold your own with other talented and strong-willed members of the executive team."[2] In order to do this, it is imperative to have good communication skills and they can be learned.

Charismatic Characteristics

Before we look at the communication process, I want to outline what scientists are beginning to understand about charismatic people. Charisma has a lot to do with communication. Ronald Riggio, PhD, a professor of leadership and organizational psychology who writes for *Psychology Today*, has been studying charisma for more than 30 years. He says that it has six main ingredients.[3] You'll see that they relate to either behaviour or communication, which of course are intrinsically linked.

Emotional Expressiveness: a talent for spontaneously and genuinely conveying feelings.

Emotional Sensitivity: the ability to read people's emotions and respond to their feelings.

Emotional Control: the ability to control and regulate emotional displays.

Social Expressiveness: good verbal communication skills and the ability to engage others in social interaction.

---

[1] Beeson, John, "Why You Didn't Get That Promotion," *Harvard Business Review*, June 2009, http://hbr.org/2009/06/why-you-didnt-get-that-promotion/ar/1

[2] Beeson, John, "Deconstructing Executive Presence," *Harvard Business Review*, August 22, 2012, http://blogs.hbr.org/cs/2012/08/de-constructing_executive_pres.html

[3] Riggio, Ph.D., Ronald E., "Charisma: What is it? Do you have it?" February 15, 2010, http://www.psychologytoday.com/blog/cutting-edge-leadership/201002/charisma-what-is-it-do-you-have-it

Social Sensitivity: a gift for reading and interpreting social situations by listening and tuning into others.

Social Control: a sophisticated social role-playing skill that allows a person to fit in with all sorts of people and make emotional and social connections.

How does your communication compare with these characteristics? Many people think they do an excellent job of communicating, but there is usually room for improvement. If you'd like to know how you measure up, take a moment to do an online test,[4] and then if you need to improve, focus on particular areas as you read through the next few pages.

The Communication Process

The communication process can be broken down into these basic steps:

a) The sender of a message has an idea that needs to be communicated and they convert it into words or actions. In the example I'll use, the sender converts their idea into words.

b) The sender then chooses a medium – for instance an email – to deliver the message to the receiver.

c) The receiver unpacks the message by reading the email and converting the words into a meaning.

d) The receiver then gives the sender feedback so that the sender will know whether or not the intended message was accurately received. (Of course to do so, the receiver needs to convert his or her idea about what the sender was saying in the email into a medium and deliver it back to the sender.)

It sounds pretty straightforward; however, there are many barriers that could affect this simple act of communication. People assume that everyone will interpret words in the same way, but there are currently about 600,000 words in the English language, with educated adults using about 2,000 words in daily conversation. For the 500 most frequently used words, there are some 14,000 dictionary meanings,[5] so you can see how messages can become distorted.

---

[4] http://testyourself.psychtests.com/testid/2151
[5] Wallace V. Schmidt et al., *Communicating Globally*. Sage, 2007

There can also be "noise" that interferes with the transmission of the message, such as spelling errors in the email. At the receiver's end, the decoding of the message can be influenced by the person's lack of attention, a bias against the sender, misunderstood words, emotional reactions, disinterest, a language barrier, etc. Even with the feedback travelling back to the sender, there could be a time delay which could also impede communication. Everyone needs to be a good communicator for the process to be successful. If we add visual and auditory cues to the mix, the process becomes even more complicated; however, the possibilities will be much richer.

A discussion about communication would not be complete without mentioning Dr. Albert Mehrabian's research on the subject which so many people quote out of context. Usually what people say is that when meeting someone for the first time:

- 7% of the first impression comes from your words
- 38% of the first impression comes from your voice
- 55% of the first impression comes from how you look, dress and behave

However, Dr. Mehrabian's research had a much narrower focus because it only examined the communication of feelings and attitudes, and not first impressions in general. He found that:

- 7% of the message pertaining to feelings and attitudes is in the words that are spoken.
- 38% of the message pertaining to feelings and attitudes is paralinguistic (the way that the words are said).
- 55% of the message pertaining to feelings and attitudes is in facial expression.[6]

In all of this, it is important to remember that your appearance, body language and voice will affect communication far more than people expect. If the nonverbal cues contradict what you are saying, they will be believed more than your actual words.

---

[6] http://www.businessballs.com/mehrabiancommunications.htm

Voice and Speech Patterns

There are several aspects of your voice and speech patterns that can be used to create connections and empower your presence.

- To create as much rapport with people as possible, match the speed of your voice with theirs. They'll immediately feel more comfortable with you. You can also use a sincere, empathetic, caring tone of voice, showing that you have the person's best interest in mind.

- If you want to be persuasive, speak with a faster tempo. Just be careful that the speed is not excessive or people will wonder what you're trying to hide or sell. As well, if you speak too fast, there is a danger that the clarity of your communication will be diminished because it would be difficult for you to properly enunciate your words.

- People are uncomfortable with silence, and when trying to get a point across, they think that they need to completely fill the air with their words. If you do this, you'll lessen the effectiveness of your communication because your audience can't digest what you're saying while you are talking. By pausing after important words and phrases, not only will you give them time to think, you will bring attention to your key points. As long as you don't overuse this device, people will listen to your every word, which no doubt will increase your presence.

- A high, whining, squeaky voice can definitely challenge your credibility, while one that has a lower tone automatically projects more authority. A high voice can be lowered with the help of a voice coach who can show you how to relax the muscles in your throat and breathe from your diaphragm. The same goes for volume. You don't want to appear like you're yelling at someone, but if you need more authority when giving a presentation, ensure that your voice can reach the back of the room.

- To keep the listener's attention, avoid speaking in a monotone. Instead, vary your volume and pitch so that your voice climbs and falls. It's very important not to end every sentence with an upward inflection, because you'll sound as if you're constantly asking for approval, rather than making strong statements. If you say the following question out loud, putting the emphasis on a different word each time, you'll see how giving more energy to certain words can alter the meaning: *"Why did you hire him?"*

- Besides tone, tempo and inflection, your grammar and sentence structure are also important to your image and communication. Your grammar is a reflection of your culture and education and a natural part of who you are, but any misuse will most definitely be noticed by people who speak precisely.

- Because your mind works much faster than your mouth, when you are passionate or excited, you may speak in broken fragments instead of full sentences. Slowing down and using full sentences will give you more time to process information, thus avoiding potential errors and you'll command attention because people will listen to you more carefully. It will also give you time to breathe which is essential to support your voice.

- It is possible for you to develop strong, effective speaking skills; however, first you need a sense of how you come across to others. If you're wondering what your speech patterns are like, record yourself delivering a presentation, podcast or piece of prose and listen to the recording. If you have any concerns, contact a speech therapist, who can assess your situation, and if necessary, suggest a plan of action that will help.

Body Language

We've already talked about appearance and how it influences first impressions and that smiling and raising your eyebrows will give you an instant "family" connection with a stranger.[7] Remembering that your body language has more influence on your communication than your voice and words, let's look at some additional facts and strategies that will help you establish more rapport with people.

Patti Wood, who is a respected body language expert with over 30 years of experience, says:

> "We have the ability to send out and read more than 700,000 different nonverbal cues... Understanding this secret language of success — our nonverbal body language and paralanguage (the nuances of the voice) — can help us communicate with others more effectively because that is how we show our truest, most honest thoughts and feelings... Since nonverbal signals

---

[7] Bowden, Mark, *Winning Body Language for Sales Professionals: Control the Conversation and Connect with Your Customer – Without Saying a Word*, McGraw Hill, 2013

are not under our conscious control, our nonverbal communication gives a more honest and revealing message. So when you understand people's body language, you can effectively figure out their motivations, and most importantly, it allows you to see into their hearts. It allows you to have super powers... Understanding body language gives us more than clarity — it gives us peace of mind."[8]

In addition, knowing what you are projecting to others through your body language is so important. The posture you adopt at a meeting, the way you carry yourself as you walk, where your arms are placed, how you move your hands, and so much more – all will affect those observing you. While what others are doing is intriguing and very helpful, what you do is even more important, because your non-verbal communication will impact others and elicit a response.

In the scope of this chapter, I'll only be able to touch upon a few of the key body language cues that can help empower your presence, leaving it up to you to do further study on this important subject that has such a power to influence people. Two noted body language experts whose work I have valued are Mark Bowden[9] and Patti Wood[10]. The more you know about body language, the more effective a communicator you will be.

There are a few essential points to keep in mind when reading body language:

1. No body movement or position in and of itself has a precise meaning. For example, the folding of one's arms could mean that the person is defensive, relaxed or simply cold.

2. You must look at the whole body, not just one aspect at a time. If the person isn't smiling, it doesn't necessarily suggest sadness but perhaps that she or he is concentrating on other things. Look at all the areas of the person's body to determine meaning.

3. Read body language in context. What topic is being discussed? Where is the meeting taking place? Who else is present? Has the person had enough sleep?

---

[8] Wood, Patti, *Snap: Making the Most of First Impressions, Body Language, and Charisma*, New World Library, 2012

[9] http://www.truthplane.com

[10] http://www.pattiwood.net

4. There are certain body language cues that you can consciously control such as your face, but just as image is from the inside out, your body language will reveal to others what the unconscious part of your brain is thinking, particularly with gestures made from the waist down, such as the direction your feet are pointing.

5. When your body language contradicts your words, your body language will be believed. For example, if you say you're excited about something, but you're slouched in a chair with an expression of boredom on your face, your mock enthusiasm will be abundantly clear.

6. People will unconsciously mirror and copy the emotions they see in you. If you know you're skilled at something and appear confident, they will also think that you are. Just like matching the tempo of a person's voice, if you mirror and match the body language of someone else, they will feel more comfortable with you.

Open Body Language

Display open body language to attract others to you. They must trust you and feel safe because if they don't the "fight-or-flight" response that is ingrained in humans will kick in.

• A welcoming expression on your face will create an instant rapport, but also leaning in towards someone and tilting your head to one side will show them that you are interested in hearing what they have to say.

• Avoid covering your neck, heart and stomach with your hands or arms because when they are exposed, this stance will send a message of vulnerability to others, showing that you're ready to share your feelings and passions.

• When your hands are relaxed and in full view with the palms open, and facing either up or away from your body, you are expressing your openness and honesty, inviting others to do the same.

Eye Contact

• Your eye contact has the power to connect you with people and strengthen your communication. It captivates and conveys that you are trustworthy, serious and open.

- To build rapport during a conversation, you need to gaze at people 60 to 70 percent of the time, intermittently looking away[11]. More than that may be intimidating and less will send all kinds of negative messages.
- When shaking hands, hold eye contact without blinking or looking away for at least three seconds, but not much longer unless your intentions are to establish a romantic relationship.[12]

Walk and Posture

- Walk confidently by using a fairly brisk pace and good upright posture, always holding your head high. If you have a disability and use an assistive device such as a cane, pair of crutches, walker or wheelchair, keep your posture as upright as possible and move intentionally to express your confidence.
- To look more attentive when seated, avoid slouching or leaning to one side.
- To have more presence when giving a presentation, come out from behind the podium and stand with your weight equally balanced over both feet and look at the audience, instead of standing with your head down or leaning to one side. Your words will be much more powerful.

Hand and Arm Movements

- If you want to create trust, according to Bowden "an energized calm, confident, and balanced effect is felt by both the communicator and the receiver" by having your hand gestures within what he calls the TruthPlane™.[13] This is done by loosely interlacing your fingers at navel level and then moving your hands 180 degrees horizontally out from that position when gesturing. It will also positively affect your voice, breathing, heart rate, energy and facial expressions. When you drop your hands below your waist, an area which Bowden calls the GrotesquePlane™, the opposite happens.

---

[11] Wood, Patti, *Snap: Making the Most of First Impressions, Body Language, and Charisma*, New World Library, 2012

[12] Wood, Patti, *Snap: Making the Most of First Impressions, Body Language, and Charisma*, New World Library, 2012

[13] Bowden, Mark, *Winning Body Language: Control the Conversation, Command Attention, and Convey the Right Message without Saying a Word*, McGraw Hill, 2010

- When speaking with someone or giving a presentation, avoid putting your hands in your pockets, behind your back, in the "fig-leaf" position, or hanging them by your sides. If you want to draw people in, use your arms to motion towards yourself instead of pushing them away.

- The more symmetry there is between the right and left sides of your body, such as equally using both hands in the same way and within the same horizontal plane, the more your message will be understood because it stimulates both sides of the receiver's brain.

- If you want people to be just as passionate about what you are saying as you are, occasionally lift your hands higher to chest level and gesture from what Bowden calls the PassionPlane™.

- Avoid visual distractions such as twisting your hair, scratching your body, adjusting your clothing, rubbing your face, twisting your ring, playing with your pen, swaying from side to side, stomping your feet, etc.

Powerful Presentations

Whether you are an executive, administrative assistant, software developer, retail sales associate, financial advisor, volunteer for a community organization, etc., you are involved with some form of formal or informal, large or small presentations. Some people naturally enjoy speaking in front of groups, while many others fear it more than death. The fear of speaking can negatively affect what people absorb from your presentations because your fear will be conveyed to them through your nonverbal communication, causing a distraction. Unfortunately, your professional success can often be limited when you avoid the very opportunities that could lead to being noticed and promoted.

If you have a fear of speaking, it is very real and was probably learned at some point early in your life. Because it was learned, the good news is that with focus, guidance, and practise in a non-threatening environment, it is possible to improve your presentations, giving you more peace of mind. In classes I've facilitated for students and professionals, when participants are persistent, they improve dramatically, even after a brief amount of presentation skills coaching. If you want to improve your skills, in addition to videos and resources online, find a presentation skills coach or join one of the many groups, such as Toastmasters, that specialize in helping with this skill set. In addition to using techniques involving your body language, voice, and words that we've already discussed, these additional points will help you the next time you give a presentation:

- When approached to give a presentation, the first question to ask is "Why?" because everything else will fall into line once you know this.

- Ask how the meeting room will be set up, what audiovisual equipment will be available, the number and makeup of the participants, and the time allotted, so that you can organize your presentation for the best impact.

- Prepare your presentation well in advance so that you have ample time to practise it out loud. You can be a novice speaker but if you are well-prepared, it will give you a certain confidence and presence that your audience will notice.

- The first step in changing things that require improvement is to find out what they are. Using a camera to record your presentation ahead of time will reveal any repetitive speech patterns, such as the use of "um," "ah," "like" and "you know," and any obvious body language distractions. Don't be surprised if what you see and hear when you play back the recording isn't what you expected.

- Ensure that your visuals are clear enough to be seen at the back of the room so as not to lose your audience.

- Learn how to use visualization and relaxation techniques to calm your nerves, especially deep breathing because it sends endorphins into your body to counteract stress.

- To help establish your credibility when required, it is best if someone reads a short speaker's introduction that you've prepared.

- At the beginning, introduce your subject and use an attention getting strategy. Promise to solve a problem, tell a story, ask an engaging question, share a shocking statistic related to your content, or cite a brief quotation. Use humour carefully and if you are as good at telling jokes as I am, avoid them all together.

- In addition to your empathetic voice and appropriate body language, establish rapport with the audience by not appearing rushed, sincerely answering questions and being available at break time.

- Make eye contact with a few people throughout the room so that you appear to be including everyone. Remember to keep you hands at the centre of your body or higher and move both hands symmetrically.

- Keep your audience with you as you move from topic to topic by telling them where you are going next in your presentation.

- Finish within the allotted time. It is particularly important to summarize your main points at the end so that the audience doesn't feel dropped. If using PowerPoint, insert a summary slide so that they never see "the black screen of death."

Effective Conversations

Conversation is becoming a dying art. People are spending more time on their own involved with social media, texting, and the internet, rather than interacting face-to-face. Families seldom gather around a dining table to eat, let alone talk after a meal, which is really reducing the ability of children to converse and read basic body language cues.

I was delighted one summer afternoon when visiting a relative at a cottage. A 12-year old boy knocked at the door and entered, looking for his cousin. When he heard that he was still in bed, instead of leaving as most young people would have done, he immediately sat down on the sofa and asked my husband and I, "Well how are you two doing?" I was taken aback because, first, having married into the family, I'd never met the fellow before, and secondly, I don't know of many people his age, or at any age for that matter, who could look so relaxed with a stranger and swing so naturally into conversation. I'm sure he'll do well in any career path because even at his young age, he already had a magnetic personality.

When communication skills tests are performed, it's usually the older age groups that perform better compared to the younger age groups, probably due to experience, and women naturally are more comfortable than men at sharing their thoughts. As well, women are better listeners, more willing to discuss things and consider other people's opinions, and good at empathizing with people and dealing with their emotions.[14] If you are a talented conversationalist, you'll certainly set yourself apart from others and add to your

---

[14] http://www.archprofile.com/corporate/releases/pr_archprofile_communication_skills_test.html

true wealth because you'll be able to quickly establish relationships and be remembered as an engaging and attractive person.

Active Listening

One of the most important things you can do when communicating is listen to others with intent and focus. If you don't respect them enough to listen, showing that their opinions are important, they'll not pay attention to you. Besides, you will miss an awful lot in life by not listening.

- Stop talking and give the speaker your undivided attention. Instead of waiting to break into the conversation or looking for an opportunity to change the subject, be totally present in the "now" so that you can really hear what the person is saying.

- Show that you're listening by using nonverbal cues, such as nodding, writing, making eye contact, being alert, and if appropriate in the context, occasionally saying "ah hah."

- Keep an open mind and avoid being judgmental or biased.

- Ask clarifying questions and reflect back your feelings and thoughts through paraphrasing. Sometimes complex issues may also require you to use dialoguing to verify your understanding of what the speaker is saying. With this technique, you repeat back to the person exactly what you hear by starting with "What you said is...." Then the speaker can either confirm that what you said is accurate or point out a particular bias. Wait until the speaker is finished before commenting and do so in a respectful, honest way without attacking.

Showing Empathy

I'm sure if you think again about the people in your life who have presence, more often than not they are empathetic listeners. Empathy involves putting yourself in the shoes of another person in order to better understand the person's emotions, feelings and situation. When you listen with empathy, the other person is aware that you understand and support them without being judgmental. This is done by your words, body language and tone of voice and it allows the speaker to open up to you without fear of being interrupted, criticized or told what to do.[15] In addition to having active listening skills,

---

[15] Salem, Richard, "Benefits of Empathetic Listening," July 2003, http://www.beyondintractability.org/bi-essay/empathic-listening

here are some points to help you be an empathetic listener:

- You need to be a sounding board, so let the other person have the floor and genuinely listen, instead of engaging in conversation with the intent to express your opinion.

- Embrace the idea that everyone is unique, and try to see things from their perspective. Don't lessen the person's concern by saying, "Eventually it should all work out." or "Everyone goes through that at some point in time."

- Ask questions to clarify confusion, but if you ask too many, the person might think that they are being interrogated.

- Don't give advice, but instead reflect back to them what you're hearing, using the dialoguing technique mentioned earlier. You may not understand how they are feeling, but you can agree that what they are experiencing is real and that you are concerned. Use your nonverbal communication to express warmth and a strong sense of caring.

Practice Plain Courtesy

- In order to avoid awkward situations and heated arguments, it is advisable not to talk about religion, politics and morality in public because they are controversial subjects.

- If you're discussing something controversial, listen to the other side, and then state your opinions with care, so as not to appear self-centred with a hardened point of view.

- Instead of breaking into a conversation, interrupting the speaker, or finishing other people's sentences, wait until they have stopped talking to state your opinion. When you're interrupted, wait for a few seconds and then return to the point you were making.

- Share the air. If you become aware that you've been monopolizing the conversation, apologize and ask the other person an open-ended question. If someone else has taken over, sometimes your complete silence will help the person realize that they've done so, but you mustn't appear rude. You can also wait for a strategic moment when an exchange of new ideas might alter the one-sided conversation.

- Be sensitive to others and include them in your conversation by avoiding any tendency to patronize or alienate people by talking down to them or explaining the meaning of words.

- Celebrate and support ethnic and cultural diversity. Don't tell or take part in ethnic jokes or make fun of people who have regional accents or expressions. Don't segregate people into categories based on race, creed, gender, sexual orientation, income or physical ability but refer to them as persons on an equal footing.

- Don't be afraid to admit that you are wrong and apologise. Unresolved conflict results in bitterness that destroys friendships and relationships.

- People with presence feel secure and are free with their praise, while those who are insecure find it difficult. When extending a compliment, don't gush or overstate it. When someone compliments you, instead of discrediting their good opinion of you, reply with enthusiasm: "Thank you. I appreciate your positive comments." Passing on a compliment demonstrates your generous spirit and connection to the world around you. For example: "Dianne, I heard about the award you received. Congratulations!"

Avoid These Conversational Pitfalls

- There are many personal questions that can be offensive to others, so restrain your natural curiosity so as not to impede communication. Don't ask about a person's age, sexual orientation, physical problem, weight, marital status, income and whether they have had cosmetic surgery or why they don't have children.

- Avoid over-sharing. Too much personal information in inappropriate contexts will only serve to embarrass and alienate people. Also be aware in cubical-style offices that your voice carries and personal details meant for someone on the other end of the telephone are broadcast much further than expected.

- Avoid bragging because it doesn't elevate your reputation. Mentioning the name of a prominent person you know is acceptable, but if it develops into a habit, it becomes 'name-dropping,' a particularly irritating, self-centred form of bragging. If someone is always dropping names, ask a few detailed questions about the prominent person. If they don't know the person well, they'll probably not mention their name again.

- Don't tell obscene jokes to impress or entertain people; it will make you seem juvenile. Profanity is not powerful, and swearing does nothing to increase your presence.

- Gossiping doesn't enhance your image, and it never respects truth or confidentiality. Refusing to participate in gossip demonstrates civility and can cause positive changes in your relationships and surroundings.

- Avoid giving unsolicited advice because people will understandably resent it. If you think that giving such advice will save someone's job or marriage, it may be worth the risk, but it must be supported with facts and be non-judgmental. Be aware that the person may still resent your good intentions.

Small Talk Made Easy

When I've polled people on their greatest concerns connected to working a room, not knowing what to say is always on the top of the list. Some people are natural conversationalists, as we see with charismatic people, while others have to work hard at finding a topic and keeping the conversation going. In addition to networking events, small talk is valuable at the start of a business meeting, while dining, at school, when staring a new job, and when socializing. Although the content may differ depending upon whether you are at a business event or on a blind date, the process is the same. Having a positive self image and sense of purpose in life helps your confidence even before you begin the process. Here are five basic steps that you can rely on to easily start and keep a conversation going:

1. Begin the process
- Make a brief, positive comment on the venue, event, office, restaurant, etc. E.g. "Isn't this a wonderful facility!"

- The other person should pick up the thread of the conversation and keep the ball rolling, so if you're on the receiving end of such a comment, respond with more than "yes." For example: "Yes it is. What do you like best…?"

2. Introduce yourself
- Use the 7-second self-introduction that you created in Chapter 3 that emphasizes the value you bring to your clients, not a boring list of your services and products, or if in a social environment, not all your hobbies and interests.

106

- Immediately ask the person's name and profession. (At a social event, ask what prompted the person to attend.)

3. Touch on topics

- Most people freeze here. If you are in touch with your environment, current events and life in general, and you concentrate on making the other person feel comfortable, you can usually find a topic to talk about. Just don't fret if the first one doesn't work. You're not a failure!

- After weather, possible topics could include business trends, positive news, leisure activities, the arts, sports, vacations, holiday celebrations, etc.

- Be careful about asking, "What do you do?" at a social event, in case the person is not employed and wishes they were. Also, tread carefully regarding subjects involving family; for a number of reasons the person might think that is too personal. It will depend greatly on the person and the context.

- People will always enjoy speaking about themselves while you play the role of the attentive listener. If someone mentions a sports team that you don't follow or a movie you haven't seen, it is quite easy to go along with the conversation for a while by asking about the game or plot line. As long as people are talking, they'll think that the conversation is going well and that you are fabulous.

4. Expand on one topic

- Once you find a topic that you can discuss, keep on talking as long as you are getting a response. Use open-end questions, listen attentively, and share the air. Here are a few open-ended questions for business environments that have been adapted from Bob Burg's book *Endless Referrals*[16]:
  - How did you get your start in your career/business?
  - What do you enjoy most about your profession/volunteer work?
  - What advice would you give someone just starting out in your business?
  - What changes/challenges have you experienced in your profession through the years?
  - What are the current trends that are affecting your business?

---

[16] Burg, Bob, *Endless Referrals,* McGraw-Hill, 2005

- How will I know if I'm talking to someone who may need your products/services?

- People are not sure if you want to hear as much as they have to tell, so they will slow down after speaking for a while, to see if you'll change the topic. If you don't want to go through the process of finding a new one at that moment, keep them talking for a few minutes longer with: "That is very interesting. Please tell me more!" (When an executive in the entertainment sector who had great difficulty with small talk learned about this strategy, he called it "pure gold.")

- When things genuinely slow down, listen for a cue that can take you in another direction. For instance, if the conversation was centred on the hockey game, you could ask, "Do you play or coach any other sports?" with the hope to segue into something you do in your leisure time and then on to another subject from there.

5. End the conversation

- Only start the process of ending the conversation when you are talking, otherwise it will appear as if you were waiting for the person to take a breath to start the process of releasing them. They may question your sincerity. Follow this process:

  - Smile and say: "It's been really interesting speaking with you about X."

  - Then say: "I've taken up enough of your time and I am sure that there are others here that you'd like to meet."

  - Then add something along these lines:

    "I look forward to seeing you again."

    "Perhaps we can continue our discussion over coffee next week."

    "Enjoy the rest of the event."

Never view small talk as a waste of time because it opens the door for more meaningful conversations. Take every opportunity to practise your small talk because the more you do, the more it will feel natural and the greater peace of mind you will have as you head out to events. Besides, with so many people finding the process stressful, by tactfully directing conversations, you can put them at ease.

Clear Written Communication

Written words can have just as much influence as those spoken, even without the nonverbal support of the voice and body language. It's not so much that the actual words have more power, but because they have longevity through memos, reports, letters, emails, and books, and virtually through blogs, websites, and social media pages. They can be mulled over, reviewed, scrutinized, shared, discussed, and debated, so they need to be right. The importance of word choice and grammar was already mentioned when talking about speech, and of course this also pertains to the written word. When you write, you immediately demonstrate whether or not you have good command of language.

Grammar and Spelling

I think we all know that software developed to check grammar and spelling only catches the most obvious mistakes, leaving the writer with a false sense of confidence that their work is perfect. Even skimming through a document may not catch everything because our brain pays more attention to the first and last letters of a word, often missing a mistake in the middle. Reading your work out loud will help to fill in missed words and commas. Purchasing a good thesaurus, dictionary and grammar manual are good investments, especially the thesaurus because it will give you so many more options than most online tools, saving you time when searching for just the right word.

Marketing Pieces

If you are not working for an organization where the marketing pieces are pre-determined, you need to pay attention to the presentation of your business cards, letterhead, newsletters, brochures, manuals, presentation slides, DVDs, workbooks, handouts, signage, website, social media pages, etc. All these are part of your personal brand. In the same way that body language can support or undermine your spoken words, the visual elements and content of these media have a great impact on establishing a strong and professional presence. Are they consistent with the message you want to convey? For example, if when you defined your personal brand, you said that quality and sophistication were important, but your stationary looks like it was turned out on a second-rate printer, there will be an obvious disconnect that will confuse people, affecting their trust in you.

Your Online Presence

Your online presence is probably one of your most influential communication instruments that you have at your disposal. With little or no investment, everyone can create a personal brand and support it through online tools. In addition to the written word and visual appearance of websites, blogs and social media pages, your domain name, email address, comments on micro-blogs, forums and discussion boards, and anything else that has sprung into existence after this book is completed, can affect your image and personal brand.

Visibility is the key to your success and in this realm it can happen instantaneously. What goes up online, even if you did not post it, must complement your personality, strengths, values and passions – everything associated with your personal brand. As such, you need to be vigilant in managing your online reputation so that the very tool that can create instant fame and presence does not do the opposite. Remember that anything you send into cyberspace has a certain permanency and "the mike is always open," so exhibit respect, restraint and responsibility when posting and sharing information.

Email Etiquette

When preparing customized training for companies, I'm always surprised that they request a segment on email, because even though it has been in use for many years, poor form, improper sentence structure, inappropriate familiarity and cryptic content are common. Realizing that every company will be different and many people have gone to other platforms such as texting, instant messaging and social media to satisfy the need for instant communication, currently in the business environment, email is still important. Compare the following guidelines to what you are doing, and if necessary, adjust your format accordingly. Remember that you can't provide visual or audio clues to help the other person interpret your emotions.

- Keep the same standards that you use when you are face to face with a person. The anonymity of electronic communication is no excuse for rudeness or abusive messages.
- Keep your messages brief, but don't be cryptic.
- A consistent signature block of about four or five lines will ensure that your name and contact information are included; it can also convey your brand message.

- Even if your company encourages using lowercase for internal memos, correct spelling, punctuation and grammar are required when sending messages outside the organization.

- At work, keep your messages related to business because you are on company time and most firms are monitoring e-mail to detect misuse. Also important to note, records are kept and email can be used in a court of law.

- USING ALL CAPITAL LETTERS IS EQUAL TO SHOUTING. Keep your tone professional.

- Unless you use encryption software, assume that online communication isn't secure. Don't write anything that you wouldn't write on a postcard.

- If you're forwarding a message, don't change the wording. If the e-mail was personal or confidential, ask the sender's permission to forward it.

- Don't click the "reply all" button unless everyone needs to hear your answer.

- Always use an appropriate subject line, and to assist with tracking messages, continue to use it on subsequent messages.

- Accurately address your email and once the message is complete, store it in your outbox while you go on to the next message. A few moments of reflection may cause you to change the content slightly, especially if you're addressing a particularly difficult situation.

- Don't expect that the message arrives instantly at its destination, or arrives at all. Email isn't invincible. If you've not received a reply in an appropriate amount of time, inquire about it by sending another polite message or use the telephone.

- Always use a salutation, making it as formal as the context requires. For example, "Dear Mr. Cheung," would be used when you don't know the person at all. "Hello" or "Hi," with or without first names attached, are always more professional than "Hey," which belongs to causal communication. When doing business internationally, become familiar with the standard forms of address used in other countries. For business, always use a complementary closing line such as "Sincerely," "Yours truly," "Best regards," "Regards," and "Cheers." (They are listed in descending order of formality.)

- In business contexts, eliminate emoticons such as ☺.

As we come to the end of this chapter, it is noteworthy that with the presence of four generations in the workplace for the first time in history that a discussion on multi-generational communications could be very advantageous. If you are going to establish relationships across generations and foster civility, knowing something about the characteristics of each will certainly improve communication as you interact with one another on a daily basis. I will be addressing this in the next chapter, along with other image and personal branding considerations that will help you have peace of mind, engage fully in life, and increase your relationships.

Chapter 7 - At A Glance

Communication is Essential for Building Rapport

Communication, whether verbal, written or nonverbal, is essential for all human connection. Poor communication is costly. When there is good communication, there are fewer misunderstandings and disagreements and people are more productive. Skillful communicators have the ability to create trust, good morale and respect with everyone around them, adding to their true wealth.

Communication Skills Can be Learned

It is possible for you to learn how to master small talk, engage in meaningful conversations, actively listen, deliver effective presentations, responsibly handle electronic messages and control your online media, so that you will always be accurately communicating your personal brand message, building true wealth and increasing your presence.

Body Language Speaks Louder than Words

When communicating, body language has far more influence on the process than words and speech patterns. It is helpful to know how to read other people's body language, but even more important is to know how to effectively use your non-verbal communication to build rapport and control the messages that people receive from you.

Market Intelligence for All Generations

Presence is never limited by the cycles of life. Whether you are starting out in your career, shifting into management, or you've retired and are moving in new circles, you can always feel comfortable, carry yourself with confidence, and capture people's attention. Of course at various stages in your life, you'll focus on different things and priorities will change; therefore, you might want to re-examine your personal brand – your true promise of value. Don't be surprised if the brand elements that you defined in Chapter 3 are still valid because they express something that is deep within you, something that is uniquely "you." However, how you express your personal brand and how your image supports your brand message through your appearance, behaviour and communication might require some different strategies as you approach new and exciting opportunities.

With people living longer, and thus working beyond the usual retirement age, there is a tremendous amount of interest in multi-generational communications. Endless research, articles, blogs, and books over the last decade or more have addressed how in the workplace the four generations (soon to be five) approach work, authority, loyalty, reward, feedback, change, etc. "The existence of the multi-generational workforce poses unique challenges to today's business environment. A lack of understanding regarding generational differences contributes to conflict within working relationships, lowers productivity, and increases turnover. More seasoned staff can become frustrated by a seemingly aloof younger generation. Younger staff can become disenfranchised with entrenched hierarchal structures. Moreover, those employees stuck in the middle can become frustrated with everyone."[1]

Some people ask about the origins of the generational identities. They are a result of common things that people experienced such as world events and changes in the economy. I'll leave it up to you to do more research into the foundational influences if desired, while in the following pages, you will find a summary of the key characteristics of the Traditionalists, Boomers, Generation X and Generation Y as found in *Loyalty Unplugged: How to get, keep & grow four generations.*[2] I will also give you a glimpse of the newest cohort, Generation Z. If you want to have peace of mind, be fully engaged with life, and build relationships, which are at the core of having true wealth and presence, a thorough understanding of each generation and their attitudes, values, characteristics and skills, will direct you in the best way to approach individuals you meet so that you are able to connect with them in meaningful ways.

Not everyone fits neatly into their generational category and there will also be overlaps. For instance, people who were born at the beginning or the end of a cohort are considered "cuspers," exhibiting characteristics of both generations, making them good mediators. Also, it is not uncommon for some people to think that they belong in another cohort. When facilitating a seminar on multi-generational communications, a young participant said that he thought he was a Traditionalist, the oldest generation. After a short discussion, it became obvious that his culture and upbringing centred heavily on respecting elders and authority, just like the Traditionalists would have experienced in their formative years. This respect of authority, coupled with the technological skills associated with his generation, will make him a more versatile person than others in his cohort.

As we go through the generational characteristics, please note that experts do not always use the same titles and dates for each cohort, so if you decide to study this issue further, you will encounter differences. What is most important is remembering that we are people first, and we all possess incredible qualities.

---

[1] Ballone, Carrie, "Consulting Your Clients to Leverage the Multi-Generational Workforce," *Journal of Practical Consulting*, Vol. 2, Issue 1, 2007, http://www.regent.edu/acad/global/publications/jpc/vol2iss1/ballone/ballone.htm

[2] Buahene, Adwoa K. & Giselle Kovary, *Loyalty Unplugged: how to get, keep & grow all four generations*, Xlibris Corporation, 2007

If we can learn to remove our generational blinders and search for these unique attributes, instead of limiting each other, we could harness the power of all the generations. If we keep the blinders on, we not only limit ourselves and everyone around us, we also limit our true wealth.

Traditionalists

Traditionalists, also called "Veterans," were born between 1922 and 1945. Many of them were affected by the great depression referred to as "the dirty 30s." They had to sacrifice a lot to get ahead, so they tend to be very frugal and expect others to similarly pay their dues. They believe work should be done in the office under close supervision during a 9 to 5 day. They usually spend their whole career with one employer and expect a good pension when they retire. They are loyal to the organization and anticipate that people in senior management know what they are doing, because otherwise they wouldn't have been promoted. They manage with a rigid, top-down style, where the chain of command is extremely important. Rules must always be respected, and their authority should never be questioned. When working in a team, they look to the senior person to make final decisions. Change is not something they embrace, especially if things appear to be working well. Work provides them with an opportunity to create a legacy and advancing up the corporate ladder is based on tenure. Traditionalists keep their personal lives private and rarely socialize with employees outside of work, unless it is at a special occasion such as a company picnic or year-end party. Currently, they are holding top management positions, own established businesses, and are retired or possibly working part-time.

Boomers

Boomers, or "Baby Boomers" as they are also known, make up the largest group, being born after World War II between 1946 and 1964. They are known as the "me" generation, because they entered the workforce with anti-establishment attitudes and a tendency to challenge authority; however, with so many Boomers competing for jobs, they soon conformed to a hierarchical way of working. The term "workaholic" was coined to describe how many in this cohort live to work. Their self worth is tied to their careers, often at the expense of their families. Because of the corporate downsizing in the 1980s and 90s when many lost their middle management positions, they are cautious when change is in the air unless they are driving it. As their self-esteem disintegrated along with their careers, work-life balance became a greater priority. Also, the idea of working for one company or in one sector all their lives was shaken and loyalty towards their teams became more important. They are people-focused and build personal relationships with their colleagues in order to strengthen their teams, and make them successful. They love face-to-face meetings, avoid conflict and look for democratic collaboration and consensus. As their parents age, wellness has become more important to Boomers, and they focus on being fit, looking young, and enjoying a good lifestyle. They are senior and upper managers, independent consultants, and business owners. Because the recession of 2008 caused many of their investments to plummet, affecting their retirement income, many Boomers approaching age 65 are not able or ready to leave the workforce.

Generation X

People in Generation X, also known as "The NeXt Generation," were born between 1965 and 1980. It is a much smaller cohort than the Boomers due to the advent of the birth control pill. Gen Xers were known as "latchkey kids," taking care of themselves after school because usually both parents worked, or they were raised by a single parent due to an increase in divorce. As a result, they are extremely independent and self-reliant. Once team objectives are clear, they prefer to work alone on projects and wonder why they have to complete work at the office. Seeing many of their Boomer parents laid off, they don't expect to be loyal to a company, and instead focus on gaining skills to remain marketable. Competency is respected far more than titles so they are quite informal with senior executives. Because they view the employment relationship as an equal partnership, they expect to give and receive comments freely. They are more loyal to their managers than their teams, often following them to new departments or organizations because they have the power to influence their careers. They are early adopters of technology and can focus on several projects at once. Rather than worrying about process and rules, they work hard, are results-oriented, and like to add value through their output. In return, they expect their managers to commit to them and their professional development. They are friends with their co-workers, often socializing with them outside of work. However, if they don't click with a colleague, they will maintain a collaborative spirit and focus on accomplishing things together. They are at ease with change because it represents an opportunity for advancement. They are honest and direct with their communication, and when managing, they could overlook emotional factors. Work is only one part of their lives, so in order to maintain a good work-life balance, many Gen Xers are self-employed entrepreneurs, freelancers, consultants, and contract workers. In corporate environments, they are waiting for the Boomers to retire from their management positions and will readily move to another company for available opportunities.

Generation Y

The members of Generation Y, also called "Millennials," were born between 1981 and 2000. Gen Y is often seen as "the entitlement generation." People in this cohort are sophisticated, educated, people focused, and are ready to take over and run things. They like work to be creative, challenging, fun and financially rewarding and enjoy working with their friends in teams. This cohort likes to multi-task, and they'll commit to contributing with zeal as long as the work is meaningful. When it isn't, they'll not hesitate to look for employment elsewhere, sometimes taking their friends with them because they like to move in packs. Like Gen Xers, they prefer to work independently and don't see the need for office attendance[3]; however, at the same time, they want supervision and frequent feedback from managers. This may be due to their "helicopter parents" who were always directing and guiding their lives. Like Gen X, titles are not important and they tend to interact casually with everyone, including senior management, because they were raised in families where their parents were "friends" with them. As their opinions counted at home and school, they expect to contribute their ideas and be listened to, no matter what their status. Technology is so much a part of their life that the lines between work and personal time are almost non-existent; they interact on a global level, often supporting causes for social change. Their techno-savvy abilities are valued competencies that will eventually move them into managing much older people where technology is considered essential.

---

[3] Schawbel, Dan, "74 Of The Most Interesting Facts About The Millennial Generation," June 2013, http://danschawbel.com/blog/74-of-the-most-interesting-facts-about-the-millennial-generation/

Generation Z

This group was born after 2000, although experts disagree on this, with some saying as early as 1990.[4] They've also not yet agreed on the cohort name, sometimes calling it "Digital Natives" or the "Net Generation" because technology and the internet have always been a part of their lives, giving them instant access to any information. They are able to use a variety of devices with ease and their friends span the globe. When 13 – 17 year olds were asked how they'd feel if the internet was taken away from them, more than 90% said that it would cause them stress.[5] Because of the internet, they are also aware of terrorism, global warming and other world-wide concerns, giving them a high level of maturity and sense of social responsibility. When communicating, they prefer texting to having a conversation. They want constant and immediate feedback, and when they problem solve, they look for quick answers rather than taking the time to make sure things are accurate.[6] They are very aware that the 2008 economic downturn has affected their families and worry about whether there will be jobs available when they are ready to go into the workforce.

The next three sections will assist the three generations that are most prevalent in the workforce today with practical strategies on appearance, behaviour and communication. If you skip to your particular generational material, remember that your needs will be unique, depending upon your personality, individual circumstances, work and social environments, and of course your personal brand elements. Also, if you are a "cusper," some of the suggestions I've made for the generation nearest to your cohort may also apply.

Market Intelligence for Boomers

Boomers continue to put their mark on everything, as in all stages of their lives. For instance, it's evident that they don't plan to age like their parents did, and so as this huge cohort heads towards retirement, popular culture

---

[4] "Consumers of Tomorrow, Insights and Observations About Generation Z," Grail Research, November 2011, http://www.grailresearch.com/pdf/ContenPodsPdf/Consumers_of_Tomorrow_Insights_and_Observations_About_Generation_Z.pdf

[5] Palley, Will, "Gen Z: Digital in Their DNA," J, Walter Thomson Company, New York, 2012, http://www.jwtintelligence.com/wp-content/uploads/2012/04/F_INTERNAL_Gen_Z_0418122.pdf

[6] Looper, Lance. "How Generation Z Works," 23 May 2011, http://people.howstuffworks.com/culture-traditions/generation-gaps/generation-z.htm

focuses on healthy eating, fitness regimens, travel, dietary supplements, cosmetic surgery, anti-aging skincare, hormone replacement, etc. If you're a Boomer still engaged in a career and want to be considered a viable option when competing with younger generations for promotions, your work alone is not enough. You need to clearly communicate the value that you bring to the organization – in effect, turning yourself into a valued commodity expressed through your personal brand. (This is not always comfortable for Boomers, given that they feel the overall teams are often more important than the part they play.) An image update will ensure that any visual distractions are minimized and important skills are polished, maintaining your self-esteem, confidence and chances of success.

Appearance

You know that appearance affects first impressions. Although there has been minimal research completed on ageism, compared to that done on race and gender biases, it would be fair to say that increased signs of aging in one's appearance will influence decisions.[7] Just like the motivation behind whether or not to apply makeup, grow a beard, wear a skirt, don a tie, etc. is very personal, some people are happy with their appearance in the latter years of their life, regardless of what others think, while others seek solutions to turn back the clock. Consequently, I don't want to assume that everyone has an interest in appearing younger. However, in my work as an image advisor, the majority of Boomers who consult with me are very concerned about aging because people make value judgements and miss their inner qualities and experience, which like good red wines, improve with age. In that light, take what you will from these suggestions:

- Seek to be "presence perfect" in every situation. You can easily look scruffy by waiting a week too long to get a haircut or colour touch up, unfit by wearing clothes that are too tight, and outdated with those 80s styles still in your closet. When choosing clothing, focus on personal style, rather than on fads or edgy fashions, so that you don't come off looking like "mutton dressed as lamb" – as if you are trying too hard to look young.

- To create the best possible environment for communication, plan your clothing strategies to reach your generational audience. For example, if

---

7 Boissonnault, Paul, "Look out! Here come the boomers: Ageism and the apocalyptic demographic," Simon Fraser University, March 2008, http://www.kwantlen.ca/__shared/assets/boissonnault_boomers7420.pdf

you're meeting with a Traditionalist, you need to be more formal than when interacting with younger people. Because Gen Xers and Gen Ys are so unimpressed with status and titles, suits will not necessarily increase your authority with them. Unless your industry or the situation requires formality, when meeting with younger generations refrain from wearing a suit or if you already have one on, remove your jacket, otherwise they may see you as that "old guy/gal." If a jacket is necessary, then wear a sports coat or a mid-coloured suit to be more approachable, as already discussed in demystifying business casual attire in Chapter 5.

- Pay special attention to the frames of your glasses, making sure that they give your face a lift. If you see that aviator glasses are back in style, the ones in your drawer that you wore the 70s may be very "retro," but if you are in your mid-50s or older, they'll probably make your face look droopy.

- As your body changes over time, the clothing styles that you can wear successfully will shift. Instead of bemoaning the fact that your physique is not what it used to be, contact an image consultant, stylist or personal shopper for some fresh and appropriate ideas. Also, consider wearing slightly looser clothing, or if you wish, use foundation garments that smooth your body.

- Because our metabolism usually slows as we age, it's important to evaluate your diet to keep your weight within a good range for your height and bone structure.

- If you colour your hair, chose a shade that is one or two tones lighter than your natural hair colour to minimize any "experience" seen in your face. A professional hair stylist will be able to direct you to the best style for your facial features and the texture of your hair.

  o Men, if you colour-enhance your hair and have a beard, don't forget to colour your beard as well. Resist the urge to comb your hair over thinning areas; instead cut your hair shorter overall. If you have little hair on the top of your head, cut the sides very short or if you want an even more youthful look, shave your head. Modern hair systems, which are very difficult to detect, are also solutions for thinning hair and wearing one can greatly increase your self-esteem.

  o Women tend to continue to wear hairstyles they had in the prime of their lives, making them appear out of touch. Updating your hairstyle will have the effect of making you more vibrant than almost anything else. If you want to reduce any marionette lines near your mouth, avoid long straight styles, especially parted in the middle.

- Less is better than more when applying makeup. Avoid frosted cosmetics and don't apply heavy eye shadow just below your brow line because it will make your eyes look tired and sad.

- A good skincare regime can help you maintain the hydration and texture of your mature skin. There are many products on the market that promise anti-aging miracles. Some are very effective when used regularly and could be alternatives to invasive injections or radical cosmetic surgery.

- Whitening your teeth will give you a fresh look; however, your teeth should never be brighter than the whites of your eyes.

- Slightly softening the colours of your attire will make you appear younger. Also if your hair has a lot of "arctic blonde" in it, you may find that wearing slightly cooler tones are more flattering than warmer ones.

- Maintain your energy level with good sleep hygiene, healthy food, and a regular fitness program to keep up with those amazing young people.

Behaviour

You may be moving in new social circles or involved in philanthropy due to retirement, inherited wealth, a change in marital status, or other priorities. In some cases, you may need to attend formal receptions and fundraising gala dinners, and depending upon the social environments you are used to, you will either be comfortable or possibly find them quite intimidating.

- If eating around a formally set dining table was not a common occurrence in past years, arrange to receive some private coaching over one or more meals with a dining etiquette professional.

- Review the steps on how to work a room in Chapter 6 and take every opportunity to practise them. In order to have presence, you need to know how to do everything involved in this activity with little or no effort.

- Shift some of the energy that you used at work to assist people in the community who need encouragement or skills, showing your true civility.

- Accept the fact that some management positions will need the skills of high-tech Gen Xers, so you may find yourself working under someone much younger. Make it clear that you're interested in having a good working relationship. If the manager sees that you are willing to share your ideas, rather than criticise, more will be accomplished. Don't expect frequent meetings; be assured that when you are left alone, you are being trusted to do your job.

- Take some time away from your workaholic tendencies and get to know younger staff, especially the Gen Y's who want to be everyone's friend. Not only does it increase rapport, they may also be your manager one day.

Communication

Keep in mind that every generation has their own preference for communication and just because it is not the same as yours, it is not ineffective.

- Connect to the contemporary environment by staying up to date with technology and social media because younger generations will respect you more. Texting is very effective in speeding up internal communications, especially with team members that work in the field, allowing projects to proceed uninhibited by delays associated with email and voicemail. Ask younger people to help you navigate the intricacies of new devices and software.

- Taking pride in your words and speaking thoughtfully will increase your presence. Don't tell stories repeatedly and avoid talking endlessly about one topic, especially describing your ailments in great detail. This will alienate you from the younger generations more than anything else because it draws attention to age gaps.

- Don't be distracted by Gen Xers and Gen Ys' minimal eye contact and what seems to you to be casual or aloof behaviour. These are not necessarily linked to a lack of interest or poor performance.

Market Intelligence for Generation X

Although many Boomers say that they will work past the age of 65, the workforce will still be faced with a huge dilemma when they begin to retire. Although the Gen Xers have been waiting for chances to move into management, due to the small size of their cohort, there won't be enough people to fill the vacant positions. You may feel that you are more than ready to take on increased responsibilities, but if you are not adequately prepared, it will be a bigger challenge than it appears to be on the surface. In order to develop the skills, attributes and confidence necessary to convince decision makers that you would be a viable management candidate, become involved in mentoring programs, participate in cross-generational teams and take on leadership roles whenever possible. Your image and presence will also play a huge role in this process.

Appearance

Gen Xers are very familiar with transition – some are hitting middle-age, others are re-entering the workforce after having children, those who were laid off are being re-educated, others are starting businesses, and as mentioned, many in large companies are hoping to move up the corporate ladder. Because Gen Xers have lived their lives in the shadow of Boomers, they need to stand out. In addition to what is covered in Chapter 5, here are some more appearance strategies to consider in order for you to have as much presence as possible:

- If traditional business attire is worn by supervisors in your organization, cultivate an image that will take you into management. Your closet should contain investment pieces such as quality suits, jackets and shirts or blouses. When they are worn for important meetings with management, clients and shareholders, Traditionalists and Boomers will see that you are responsible and prepared for the next level.

- The body changes associated with childbirth or middle age are concerning for some. Instead of criticising your physique, seek professional help for new clothing options that will make you feel good about yourself. I find that people re-entering the workforce after a time at home feel particularly vulnerable and that an image update always increases their self esteem and confidence so that they can concentrate on the business at hand.

- If you are a consultant, entrepreneur or business owner, your image should never be an afterthought. Align your appearance with your branding and marketing messages so that everything is unified and strong; you will be heard above the crowd and be remembered.

Behaviour

It is important to have a good grasp of the etiquette and manners that we covered in Chapter 6 because knowing what to do in all circumstances will give you a certain advantage over others who don't possess these skills. With that comes a peace of mind when interacting with people and an ability to handle unexpected situations with ease. Also, your independence and lack of respect for titles can make you appear aloof, so showing consideration for other people will be very important if you want to make meaningful connections, especially with the older generations. You'll find these tips helpful if you have a desire to move into management or if you are already there:

- Offer to run meetings whenever possible. The more responsibility you take on at work, the more it influences Traditionalists and Boomers' perception of you. Remember they love face-to-face meetings and with Boomers teams are very important, so if you can use good team building skills when leading meetings, it will also help you earn more respect.

- Boomers like to be acknowledged for their experience and wisdom; they are also competitive. When you are managing them, instead of telling them what to do, emphasize the win-win components of any projects, involve them in the processes, and ask for their input so that they will buy into what you are proposing.

- Consider volunteering in the community and take on positions of leadership within organizations where others will see your strong qualities. It could help you establish rapport with other potential managers who might consider you for future employment.

- Polish your social skills so that a lack of know-how will not impede your communication and image, whether at work, in the community, or during lunch interviews which are often conducted when filling management positions.

- Given that you prefer to interact casually with everyone, this could be misinterpreted as disrespect by older generations. If you need to connect with Traditionalists or Boomers, take every effort to show politeness and deference, leaving aside your judgment as to whether they deserve it or not. With Traditionalists, respect the rules and processes as well.

- Although your goal is often to achieve output through projects, show some interest in the organization (for the Traditionalists), the team (for the Boomers) and your colleagues (for Generation Y). Collaborating and building relationships with people at all levels will not only allow you to be a good mediator when opportunities arise, it will also enhance your true wealth.

Communication

Boomers and Traditionalists will expect you to set an example for Gen Ys. Because your communication style tends to be honest and direct, be careful not to overlook the emotions of other people. Review the sections on active listening and empathy in Chapter 7 and then consider these points:

- When speaking with Traditionalists, make good eye contact, display attentive posture and defer to them. After they have spoken, carefully and respectfully share your views. If the environment is noisy, use enough volume without shouting because 55% of seniors have some form of hearing loss.[8] (30% of teens do as well.[9])

- Establish good connections with everyone at work. To elevate your top-of-mind awareness like any brand manager, acknowledge colleagues you pass in the hall, join people for lunch, and have meaningful conversations while you wait for meetings to start.

- Although you will likely prefer to use email to address difficult subjects, it is better to pick up the phone or arrange a meeting so that communication is effective, especially when emotional issues are involved.

- Use proper email format when communicating with Boomers; text Gen Ys unless you need a paper trail. If Traditionalists haven't embraced technology, a quick memo delivered to their desk, a telephone call or a short meeting would be effective. Of course, Boomers love meetings as well.

- When managing Boomers, make sure that you communicate frequently enough with them so that they feel at ease, because you'll probably have less face-to-face meetings than is comfortable for them.

Market Intelligence for Generation Y

Because Generation Y is perceived as "the entitlement generation" and mature, experienced Traditionalists and Boomers expect their opinions to have more validity, Gen Ys are often up against a credibility challenge. You are educated, techno-savvy and ready to take on tasks as equal members of the

---

[8] http://www.statcan.gc.ca/pub/82-003-x/2004004/article/8044-eng.pdf

[9] Statistics, The Hearing Foundation of Canada, http://www.thfc.ca/cms/en/KeyStatistics/KeyStatistics.aspx?menuid=87

team, but to be trusted, you must win the confidence of the older generations who usually control what happens in the workplace, at least for a while longer. Think about these strategies and how they might help you:

Appearance

When entering the workforce, Gen Ys must contend with the stereotypical opinions of older generations that associate a certain appearance with professionalism, and because you're unimpressed by authority, you'll probably not see the value in dressing formally. Dress codes will vary with each sector and organization, with information technology still being quite relaxed, so you need to assess what is expected. However, when competition becomes tight, such as in an economic downturn, even in the most casual industries dress codes become more important because companies want to use every advantage they have to win credibility, clients, and contracts. Study the context of your workplace and then apply the most appropriate image strategies, keeping in mind these ideas:

- Many Gen Ys want to look older as they transition from school to work so that they will be taken seriously. The most important thing you can do is to dress well early in your career. (Thoroughly study Chapter 5 for specific details.) If you want to get ahead, you need to always look like you are ready to take care of the organization's best client, should they happen to arrive unexpectedly.

- What you can wear to the beach, bar or bed should not come to work. Traditional business attire in some fields will not be expected, but the well-known strategy of dressing for the position that you want to obtain certainly counts here. Also, by giving some thought to your attire and grooming, you convey your professionalism and avoid those embarrassing "courageous conversations" about appearance and grooming that everyone dreads.

- The more unusual or eccentric your outward image is, the stronger your personality needs to be, because you'll have to work harder to convince people to take you seriously. Wearing clothes that are considered "appropriate" for the situation will send a message that you respect the values of the organization and want to be involved. There are plenty of opportunities to have fun with fashion outside of work.

- Less is more. When dressing casually, wear fewer colours for more authority. With traditional attire, wear fewer accessories so that they don't distract. When choosing a wardrobe, buy a few classic pieces that can coordinate, stretching your clothing dollars and positively impacting the environment.

- Don't borrow clothing for an interview because you can't have it altered to fit. You will feel confident in something moderately priced as long as it fits, is well-pressed, is appropriate for the environment and you like it.

- Once you are successful in gaining a position, make sure to maintain the same image that your hiring manager saw at your interview.

- Ask the professionals at a hair salon or barber for assistance with your hairstyle and colour, keeping it appropriate for your personal brand and workplace.

- Young women appear more mature and polished if they wear makeup as long as it is applied with care and appears natural.

- Avoid wearing head coverings indoors unless one is necessary for religious reasons.

- Body piercings and tattoos are very personal expressions of individuality. In spite of their popularity, be sensitive to situations where they could create a barrier to communication, especially in conservative environments and when interacting with Traditionalists.

Behaviour

When you exhibit "appropriate" behaviour and decorum across a wide variety of contexts, it will increase your maturity and presence. Of course, what is "appropriate" is usually based on the expectations of Traditionalists and Boomers who feel they have earned the right to call the shots.

- Although you want to get ahead quickly, have patience with Traditionalists and Boomers. Because they know that you thrive on change and you wouldn't hesitate to move to another organization for new opportunities, they might hesitate to invest in you at first due to the tremendous cost associated with training. Let them see that you are truly committed and ask for more responsibility once you have gained their trust.

- When interacting with people at work, see them as internal clients and apply any customer service skills you might have gained through previous employment.

- Older generations think that you expect everything to be handed to you, so you need to prove to them that you are cooperative and have initiative. To help dispel this myth, when you've completed your assigned tasks, ask to assist with other work or find something productive to do.

- Although you like to work with your friends, offer to join other teams to add your expertise where is it most needed.

- You'll gain a lot of presence if you don't address Traditionalists by their first names until they give you permission to do so.

- During work hours, use your break times to text your friends because older generations will expect that work is work, and play is play.

- Many organizations support community fundraising events. Volunteer your time to gain visibility and to prove that you have good organizational skills, can be responsible and are able to run things effectively.

- Find out what qualities are important for leadership so that you can begin to develop and use them before you actually become a manager. The more you know about Boomers and Gen Xers and why they act the way they do, the better a manager you will be.

Communication

You know that good communication is important for developing and maintaining relationships that contribute to true wealth. Your communication style is going to be very immediate compared to other generations because you've always been encouraged to express your ideas, no matter what the circumstances. Even so, studies show that young people are not as skilled at communication compared to more mature people.[10] To help you develop these skills, review Chapter 7 and then listen to Traditionalists and Boomers speaking. Notice the vocabulary they use and how they express their thoughts. Also, watch how their body language supports their ideas and creates connections with other people. Here are some additional aspects of communication to consider:

- Don't be too relaxed, familiar or blunt when communicating with older people. Instead of saying to a Traditionalist, "I don't think your idea will

---

[10] "Psychtests' New Study On Communication Skills Reveals That Women Truly Have The Gift Of Gab," Montreal, May 10, 2010, http://www.archprofile.com/corporate/releases/pr_archprofile_communication_skills_test.html

work," try: "*That may have worked well for the company in the past* (a positive comment that shows you are a team player); *however* (never use "but" because it negates the other person's idea), *with the new developments in technology that I can show you* (indicating your willingness to share your expertise), *I think we can save money* (Traditionalists will love this!), *and get the job done faster* (and this too!) *if we...* (then reveal your incredible idea)."

- Use proper spelling, grammar, capitalization and punctuation in all written workplace communications.

- To show that you are totally present with the person you're speaking with, turn off your cell phone, make eye contact, and occasionally nod to show that you're listening.

- If you need to use your cell phone during a meeting to gather some details relevant to the work at hand, at a convenient time, tell the others present what you are doing so that they don't misinterpret your actions as inattentiveness.

- Let your manager know what kind of feedback you need in order to be successful and how you'd prefer to receive it. Also, if you are open to mentoring ask for it; it will show that you are dedicated to your job.

- When looking for employment, ensure that the message on your cell phone will give a potential employer a good impression of you if they call to set up an interview.

- If you're facing a telephone interview, which many companies use to shorten a long list of applicants or accommodate candidates who live a distance from their office, be mindful that your energy level is just as important as your answers. You'll sound more enthusiastic if you stand and move about while you're talking.

- It is easy to empower your presence online. You can market yourself through your website, social media, blog, and other communications and influence people around the world, motivating them into action with just a few key strokes. Carefully handle this power because just as you can use it to rise quickly to the top, it can also go the other way. Research showed that 91% of employers polled used social media to check out potential job candidates and 69% of them rejected a candidate based on what they saw online.[11] You will want to make sure that what is on the internet truly represents your best qualities, supporting your personal brand and adding to your overall presence.

As you encounter people throughout your day, take a moment to consider their generational background, not with the intention of putting a label on them and confining them to a box, but to understand them in order to use the most appropriate communication approach. People will enjoy interacting with you, remember you, and look forward to seeing you again – signs that you have an empowered presence.

Chapter 8 - At A Glance

Presence is Not Limited by Life Cycles

Whether you are starting out in your career, shifting into management, or you've retired and are moving in new circles, you can always feel comfortable, carry yourself with confidence, and capture people's attention. Relying on a trusted and deliberate framework for appearance, behavior and communication is key to empowering your presence.

Bridge the Generations with Understanding

Having a good understanding of the attitudes, values, characteristics and skills of Traditionalists, Boomers, Generation X, Generation Y and Generation Z will improve your insights, enhance your relationships and empower your presence.

Harness the Power of All the Generations

What is most important in multi-generational communication is remembering that we are people first, and we all possess incredible qualities. If we can learn to remove our generational blinders and search for these unique attributes, instead of limiting each other, we could harness the power of all the generations, empowering everyone's true wealth potential.

---

[11] Sundberg, Jorgen, "How Employers Use Social Media to Screen Applicants," 2013, http://theundercoverrecruiter.com/infographic-how-recruiters-use-social-media-screen-applicants/

Empowering Financial Behaviours

This book would not be complete without discussing money, the state of the financial industry, and in particular how wealth advisors can use their personal brand and image to establish positive connections with clients. In Chapter 2, we spent some time looking at true wealth and how people equate it with having meaningful relationships, being fully engaged with life and possessing peace of mind. Even though everyone I asked about their definition of true wealth said it had nothing to do with money, unless barter or non-traditional forms of currency are used, some monetary resources are essential to have a reasonable quality of life. However, the negative emotions attached to money – fear and greed – can derail the ultimate rewards of true wealth: peace of mind.

The good news is that fear can be offset with the right professional advisory team providing a strategic framework and process for consistent wealth management, and the frequent and reliable communications that enable responsible decision making. Greed, however, requires introspection. How much money is enough to empower your presence now and in the future? To what degree does a negative attachment to money impact your true wealth potential? Taking some time to reflect on what money and wealth mean to you before meeting with a tax or financial advisor will provide a framework for discussion and ongoing decisions.

Let's look at how the financial sector defines wealth. The Institute for Preparing Heirs suggests this: "Wealth includes resources and assets in all forms, from cash to bonds to ownership interests, real property, even family name, reputation, experience and intellect, as well as education of all family members and spouses, and their influence in the community."[1] As you can see, here too, wealth encompasses far more than just money.

What effect has the 2008 recession had on the financial industry? It certainly is not 'business as usual.' The global financial crisis brought economic news to the mainstream and as individuals watched the value of the investments they expected to use in their retirement plummet, they became more involved in their financial wealth management:

How are investors feeling now? According to a 2011 study, wealthy clients are "cautious, smart, less trusting and loyal and now are demanding better service and clearer value. Clients are taking nothing for granted and are probing the fundamentals of their advisor relationship: 'Do you really provide a value add for me?' and 'So why exactly should I be loyal to you?' "[2] Other research published by Bain & Company in the same year found that "customers increasingly expect more from their wealth managers in terms of information, education, guidance, advice, product choice and service levels."[3] In 2012, another study done by Northstar Research Partners and Sullivan showed that although affluent investors' trust is slowly increasing compared to 2011, the likelihood of clients to recommend their advisors to others dropped from 25% to 15%.[4] The study also found that "an advisor's ability to communicate effectively has become a key determinant in client retention because respondents reported that they were just as likely to have fired an advisor for poor communication as for poor performance; while 35 % had forgiven an advisor for a poor investment choice, only 16% had forgiven insufficient or ineffective communications."

Clients want to have closer relationships with their financial advisors, hear from them more often, and take active roles in directing their own financial futures. At the same time, they want the expertise of wealth managers to

---

[1] http://www.preparingheirs.com/about-us/our-process.php

[2] "Anticipating a new age in wealth management," Global Private Banking and Wealth Management Survey 2011, http://www.pwc.com/ca/en/banking-capital-markets/publications/anticipating-a-new-age-in-wealth-mangement-2011-10-en.pdf

[3] "Winning in wealth management," Bain & Company, April 2011, http://www.bain.com/publications/articles/winning-in-wealth-management.aspx

[4] "New Study Shows Affluent Investor Trust Increasing," Northstar Research Partners and Sullivan, October 2012, http://www.northstarhub.com/blog/syndicated/investor-trust-study/

guide them. While you are expected to give better and more frequent one-on-one advice, due to the aftermath of the economic crisis, there is equal pressure to comply with new regulatory accountability standards, requiring increased hands-on work behind the scenes. To assist with this added workload, clients' records and communication, you will likely be faced with the usage of new technology, and if you are a Boomer, a sharp learning curve.

To add to this, over the next 35 years, the world will see the largest amount of wealth ever transfer from one generation to the next. Not only the expertise of financial institutions, wealth managers, accountants, lawyers, and tax specialists will be needed, but also consultants, meeting facilitators, educators, family coaches, and psychologists will be involved to make this wealth transfer successful. If you are a financial professional, in addition to possessing the skills necessary to deal with wealth management, it's critical for you to maintain relationships with existing clients. Far in advance of any transfer, you also need to establish good connections with heirs and those who have never had a financial advisor before. Communication needs to be at the forefront of what you do because only one out of every two clients in the 30 – 49 age group, that stands to inherit from the Boomers, is satisfied with their primary wealth provider.[5] The more you know about what your clients think about you and your services, the more you can customize the way you do business to maintain their trust. Sometimes you might feel like a chameleon as you develop unique financial plans for each situation, but in the end, it will net positive results.

Financial Literacy is a Must!

To build on the capital accumulated by the current generation, there is an urgent need for everyone in the family to be financially literate and familiar with the guidelines that form joint decisions with tax and financial advisors. Financial service providers will play very important roles as educators in the next few years. In an effort to increase financial literacy, younger clients will be expected to take control of their financial futures in ways that Boomers never even imagined. Evelyn Jacks, President of Knowledge Bureau and a member of Canada's Federal Task Force on Financial Literacy, points out:

---

[5] "The "Greater" Wealth Transfer: Capitalizing on the Intergenerational Shift in Wealth," Accenture, 2012, http://www.accenture.com/SiteCollectionDocuments/PDF/Accenture-CM-AWAMS-Wealth-Transfer-Final-June2012-Web-Version.pdf

"Since the unfolding of the financial crisis, financial literacy has been globally acknowledged as a key life skill according to the OECD [Organization for Economic Co-operation and Development].[6] Increasingly, more responsibility for future financial well-being and financial decision-making is shifting from governments and the private sector onto the individual and families. Financial education is required and is critical in improving financial behaviors overall and a key driver in developing rapport and connection with clients to facilitate financial planning..."Since the unfolding of the financial crisis,... More than any other single issue, we heard that the challenges of financial literacy affect every Canadian and bind us together in our mutual need for self-improvement. Financial illiteracy is the one issue that everyone can agree on: in a constantly changing financial world, improving here will help secure futures. Increasingly, as we see more responsibility for future financial well-being shifting to the individual, financial education is required to make confident decisions. An important new role of future financial advisors therefore emerges: that of educator, advocate and steward."[7]

Facilitating Financial Literacy:

• As you continually upgrade your skills, ensure that you include courses on family estate planning, so that you are equipped to educate clients and help them through the transitions ahead.

• Be particularly aware that Gen X and Gen Y will come to you with more financial knowledge than previous clients because of the internet. As well, Gen Y will readily share such information with their peers and rely heavily on their opinions to make decisions.

• Generation X's desire to manage and control their futures, coupled with a lack of trust of formal institutions, have translated into Gen Xers being one of the largest groups of financial investors because they don't expect the government to bankroll their retirement.[8] Study their generational

---

[6] OECD/INFE High-Level Principles on National Strategies for Financial Education, August 2012

[7] Jacks, Evelyn, Knowledge Bureau White Paper, Winnipeg, MB, 2013

[8] Buahene, Adwoa K. & Giselle Kovary, *Loyalty Unplugged: How to get, keep & grow all four generations*, Xlibris Corporation, 2007 (176)

characteristics to understand them and be ready to assist with their financial literacy.

- Become known as "the financial literacy expert" through developing and marketing a series of educational tools customized to reach people at various stages in their lives. In addition to traditional presentations at schools, service clubs, community groups, etc., younger generations will respond well to webinars, videos, podcasts, and other online tools to access this information.

- Be available for media interviews, call-in shows, weekly financial reports, and hosting charity events to gain more visibility, of course making sure that your image is presence perfect.

- Newly inherited wealth can cause great stress for many if they don't have a professional team in place to guide them, especially if they are lacking in financially literacy. They may even be embarrassed. If you can pull together the people necessary to assist with the wealth transfer, they will be grateful and your presence in their lives will be increased.

- Wealthy clients are not only concerned about the actual transfer of wealth but passing on to their heirs their values in relation to wealth so that it is handled responsibly.[9] Conveying these values is also a part of financial literacy. Encourage clients to talk to heirs about their financial values and to be good role models in all circumstances – actions always speak louder than words.

- Younger generations already demonstrate concern for good causes, so you want to encourage and build on this. Suggest that clients involve their heirs in philanthropy, by giving them a modest amount of money to donate to an organization of their choice, and taking them to community fundraisers, rather than simply writing cheques.

- If young people are taught how to start conversations, as well as the proper etiquette for formal affairs, they'll enjoy themselves and their confidence will be increased. Besides, they've already "aced" social networking; with a bit of direction, face-to-face interaction will not be that difficult and it will make them more well-rounded individuals.

---

[9] Williams, Roy & Vic Preisser, *Preparing Heirs: Five Steps to a Successful Transition of Family Wealth and Values,* Bandon, OR: Robert D. Reed Publishers 2003 & 2012.

Start with Customer Advocacy

Customer advocacy is the perception on the part of customers that a firm does what is best for them, not just what is best for the firm's own bottom line. Research shows that when customers feel financial service firms act in their best interests, they are willing to invest more, borrow more and buy more products from that firm.[10] Small companies are better at doing this than large ones and when financial service providers actively focus on what customers need and deliver it, they are more effective.[11] Some clients favour working with advisors who are "independent" because they are not beholden to product manufacturers.[12] If you work for a large firm, creating close relationships with your clients will help to increase their loyalty, not only with you, but with the company, ensuring a long and happy business life for everyone. So how can you be seen as a client advocate?

Establishing Client Relationships:

- In order for your clients to feel that you are honest and sincere and have their best interests in mind, your first goal is to make comfortable, meaningful connections with them. As we discussed in Chapter 4, making good first impressions through your image is vital when establishing rapport. When people hear that I'm an image consultant, it's as if I have the power to magically transform strangers I've never met. Invariably, they suggest that I ask people in financial institutions to do away with business casual dress and revert back to traditional business attire. They hate seeing their wealth managers dress down. If people are investing with you, they are also investing in a relationship with a professional, and they like it when you look the part. Taking regional differences into account, when handling money, it is important to dress as formally as the environment will allow.

---

[10] "Customer Advocacy Q2 2012: How US Consumers Rate Their Financial Services Firms," http://www.forrester.com/Customer+Advocacy+2013+How+Customers+Rate+US+Banks+Insurers+Investment+Firms+And+Credit+Card+Issuers/fulltext/-/E-RES86881?aid=AST936611

[11] "Winning in wealth management," Bain & Company, April 2011, http://www.bain.com/publications/articles/winning-in-wealth-management.aspx

[12] "Winning in wealth management," Bain & Company, April 2011, http://www.bain.com/publications/articles/winning-in-wealth-management.aspx

- Be polite, reliable and punctual with your appointments, proving to your clients that they are your first priority.
- As Mark Bowden describes in his book *Winning Body Language for Sales Professionals,* [13] to make strong connections with people, you need to be purposeful with your body language because it has such a powerful affect on a subconscious level. Your intention should not be to manipulate your clients, but rather recognise that non-verbal communication will always take place and if you use it to create a safe, relaxed environment, clients will be more apt to trust you and open up. Here are a few of his recommendations:
  - There is always tension associated with talking about money. According to Bowden, smiling can relieve tension. Remember that it also sends a subconscious message to others that you are a "friend," and when you slightly raise your eyebrows they'll feel that you are "family."
  - Create a natural sense of calm by sitting so that your stomach, a vulnerable part of your body, is in view and you are able to gesture from the TruthPlane – the area near your navel. Simply pushing your chair back from a desk will allow you to do this.
  - Tilt your head to one side and slightly lean towards the other to show that you are interested and paying attention.
  - While you are telling your client that you are looking forward to working with them, bring your hands with your palms open towards your body to draw the person closer.
  - If your office is large enough, come out from behind your desk and sit on a couch or two chairs so that you are at 90 degrees to each other rather than being across from one another, which can be confrontational.
  - Sitting at a round table is also excellent because it creates a collaborative spirit, especially when you are with two or more people.
  - In a boardroom, if you want your client to have the seat of power, invite the person to sit at the head of table and take the first seat on one of the long sides to allow you to push your chair back from the table, removing any physical barrier between the two of you.

---

[13] Bowden, Mark, *Winning Body Language for Sales Professionals: Control the Conversation and Connect with Your Customer – Without Saying a Word,* McGraw Hill, 2013

- o Avoid covering your mouth with your hands as you talk because it will frustrate your listeners if they can't see your lips.
- o If you are meeting with two people and one is more dominant, turn your body towards the quiet one in order to encourage them to participate.
- o If you are meeting your client in their home, be extremely careful because you are invading their territory. Until they get to know you, they'll be quite cautious.

- Having good social intelligence (SI), which is the ability to get along well with others and to get them to cooperate with you,[14] will help you create meaningful relationships with clients. SI is a relatively new science and you can learn how to enhance your SI to help you to recognize feelings in yourself and other people, to understand what's going on in social situations, and to connect with others.

- Ensure that your marketing materials clearly and prominently communicate to clients that their needs come first. This has been very effective for other wealth advisors.[15]

- Due to Gen X's tendency to be independent and skeptical as a result of seeing their Boomer parents laid off, initially they may not trust your intentions. However, just as they form close alliances with their supervisors (because of their power to positively affect their careers), if they clearly see that their financial security is your first priority, it will be easier to forge a close relationship with them.

- Once Gen Ys get to know you, they'll want to be your friends, until then keep in mind that the alliances they have with their peers may influence whether they trust you or not. Due to the instant gratification technology provides them, if they are not financially literate, they could expect to see immediate and unrealistic growth in their investments. Once you've gained their trust, ask to spend sufficient time with them and their peers to explain how things work.

---

[14] Albrecht, Karl, *Social Intelligence: The New Science of Success,* San Francisco, CA: Jossey-Bass, 2006

[15] "What wealth management firms can learn from Forrester's 2013 Customer Advocacy Report," http://recombo.com/2013/07/wealth-management-customer-advocacy-customer-experience/

Create Strong Client Experiences

Once your clients know that their best interests are uppermost in your mind, you need to reinforce this with positive customer experiences. If done consistently and in genuine ways, loyalty will be increased over time and clients will be more likely to recommend you to colleagues and friends.

Reinforcing Your Client Connections:

- Instead of pushing your agenda or product, which would be so obvious to clients, deliver what they need.

- Ask your client how and when they would like you to follow up and be sure to adhere to their request.

- Show sensitivity when working with someone with an unfamiliar cultural background.

- When working with senior clients, ask them what time of day is best for them, without being condescending.

- Confidentiality is essential in your work. A lack of it will not only compromise your client's information but it will erode their trust in you and make others who overhear the private information very uneasy. In offices with thin walls or dropped ceilings, use a white noise machine to keep conversations from drifting into other areas of the office.

- Invite clients to events especially created for their education or enjoyment, without an underlying agenda to "sell" to them.

- If you change firms and your clients want to follow you, make the transition easy for them. Recently, I had to transfer the processing of my credit card sales to another firm. I approached a few companies to compare their services and the inability of salespeople to succinctly summarize details so I could make a quick, informed decision was frustrating. The third person I spoke to was amazing. Without being patronizing, she clearly explained the various options, the associated fees, and then more than once, she assured me by saying: "I'm going to make this process easy for you." – and then she did.

- Invest in technology that will enable you to communicate with clients who favour using smart phones, tablets, and other mobile devices. The easier you make communication, the happier they will be. Younger clients will also expect to have online access to their investment portfolios.

- Having a meal with your clients can be one of the most effective ways to establish close relationships, because there is something about gathering around a dining table that gives you quality time to get to know each other better. We've already covered dining etiquette in Chapter 6, so here are the guidelines associated with hosting a business lunch:
  - Invite your client to lunch at least a week ahead of time and give them a choice of two restaurants. Make reservations if possible, and ask for a private table if you have important business matters to discuss.
  - Arrive at the restaurant 20 minutes early to ensure that you are there before your guest and that the table is suitable. Don't touch anything on the table until they arrive. If your guest doesn't appear within 20 minutes of the agreed-upon time, call them. If after 30 minutes they haven't come, either order your lunch or leave. If you choose to leave, give the server a generous tip.
  - If you are delayed, call your client's cell phone or let the restaurant know so that they can convey the message and offer your guest a drink or an appetizer.
  - When your guest arrives, stand up and shake hands. (If you walk in together, let them walk ahead of you to the table.) Offer them the best seat, and if you are dining with more than one person, seat the guest of honour on your right. Confirm how much time they have for the meal.
  - Invite your guest to order first and if they order a drink, soup, an appetizer, or dessert, keep them company by doing likewise.
  - Avoid ordering foods that are difficult to eat such as seafood in the shell, spaghetti, artichokes and French onion soup. Sometimes, the effort and skill you need in order to eat these dishes gracefully would be better spent discussing business.
  - After your orders are taken, conversation can turn to business unless your discussion involves a laptop, tablet or paperwork. In this case, wait until after the meal, when the table has been cleared.
  - Don't complain about the food, the restaurant or the wait staff. If your guest requires anything ask the wait staff to assist.
  - Pace yourself so that you eat at the same speed as your guest, finishing the meal within the scheduled time.

- As host, you're expected to pay the bill, with no contribution from your guest. If there is an error on the bill, speak to the server after they've gone.
- Escort your guest to the door and thank the person for coming. If you've used the coat check, tip the attendant for both coats.

- In addition to the messages that your personal appearance will send to others, your environments will also reflect and reinforce who you are.[16] Your office is an extension of your personal brand and it will tell your clients a tremendous amount about you, so ensure that the message is accurate. Because you become used to your surroundings, you may need a second set of eyes to really see your premises as people would when visiting you for the first time. Think about how the following can be used to create positive first impressions and contribute to stellar client experiences:
  - Just like curb appeal has a lot to do with selling a house, what people see as they approach your building and enter will affect their expectations of you. A financial advisor asked me to assess the first impression of the firm's facility, staff, and marketing materials. My initial reaction was positive because there was designated guest parking, the grounds and gardens were neatly groomed, and the front glass door was free of smudges. Once inside, I came face to face with a wall covered by a gigantic, gloomy modern oil painting done in very dark, muddy colours depicting menacing factories and industrial cogs against a dark steel grey sky. On either side of the painting were rows of chairs, creating a waiting area. It was obvious to me that the owners, who wanted to convey an upscale image, had gone to the expense of installing original art in the lobby, but spending any length of time there would strip away any positive feelings that clients might have upon arrival.
  - Here are some additional questions to ask yourself:
    ~ How does your "director of first impressions" (reception staff) appear and are visitors greeted warmly and professionally?
    ~ Do you have client washrooms or do they have to share the facility with the mop and bucket that has nowhere else to go?

---

[16] http://psypress.co.uk/smithandmackie/resources/topic.asp?topic=ch03-tp-01

~ Is the coat closet tidy or is there a pile of old shoes and boots on the floor?

~ Do the walls or trim need a coat of paint? Are the carpets clean?

~ Do the staff areas that clients pass on the way to your office look businesslike or are they cluttered with too many personal items?

~ Does your office appear organized and inviting? (If you like to work with files everywhere, take your clients into a meeting room so that they are not distracted by your "organized chaos.")

~ If you travel to clients, what impression does your mode of transportation make?

~ If you have to drive a customer somewhere, is your car tidy and clean or does it smell of last evening's take-out?

These questions probably sound very elementary. The point is – even the smallest detail can send doubt about you into your customers' minds. They may hesitate to recommend you to others or even worse, contemplate going to one of your competitors. You need to do everything in your power to avoid negative impressions because as you know, they are almost impossible to change.

Operation Wealth Transfer

One of the most important responsibilities wealth advisors will have over the next several years is assisting families to transfer their wealth from one generation to the next. According to Knowledge Bureau's white paper,[17] "the biggest worry for the very rich in Canada is that their children will squander the family fortune[18]. There is good reason, because inheritors do tend to bypass professional help. A July 2009 study by BMO found that of those aged 65 or older who had received an inheritance, 75% did not speak to an advisor; of those age 45 to 65, 80% did not engage an advisor.[19] Worse, in a study dated March 30, 2011, 25% of investors under 50 switched advisors within

[17] Jacks, Evelyn, Knowledge Bureau White Paper, Winnipeg, MB, 2013

[18] Census Research of 165 Canadians worth more than $10 Million.

[19] "Passing it on: What will future inheritances look like?" BMO Financial Group, July 2009

the immediately preceding two years, while 33% more planned to leave their advisors in the next year[20]."

The statistics on the wealth transfer process are staggering. According to Roy Williams and Vic Preisser in their book *Preparing Heirs,* 70% of wealth transitions worldwide fail. The research they conducted to find out why this happens concluded that:

- 60% of the transition failures were caused by a breakdown of communications and trust within the family unit
- 25% of the failures were caused by inadequately prepared heirs
- 15% of the failures were attributed to all other causes, such as tax considerations, legal issues, mission planning, etc.[21]

I'm sure that you're wondering about the role that wealth advisors played. The failures of financial professionals to correctly interpret (or anticipate) taxation, governance, and wealth preservation were only responsible for less than 3% of the wealth transition failures.

True wealth requires a framework for managing the link between financial assets, personal and family health, and collective peace of mind. Families need assistance to transfer their wealth using orderly well-thought out processes, which in the end will result in a sense of completeness and assurance for so many people, both young and old. In addition to having a wide range of wealth-specific professional skills, you need to empower your own personal brand and image to build trust, establish meaningful relationships and provide exceptional client experiences across generations. This will not only solidify current client relationships, but it will also create top-of-mind awareness with potential clients so that you become their wealth advisor of choice.

When you did the personal branding exercises in Chapter 3, if you focused in a general way on defining your strengths, personality, values and passions, you may want to redo the exercises with your profession in mind. Your top five brand elements may change. You can then align your brand message more closely with who you are in a professional context and clearly convey

---

[20] Cisco's Internet business Solution Group, March 30, 2011

[21] Williams, Roy & Vic Preisser, *Preparing Heirs: Five Steps to a Successful Transition of Family Wealth and Values*, Bandon, OR: Robert D. Reed Publishers, 2003 & 2012.

how you can customize clients' financial strategies. Your social media profiles, the organizations you join, your volunteer efforts, and it goes without saying, your ABCs – appearance, behaviour and communication – all need to be in line with your brand message and the client brand experience for you to establish trust and have the greatest impact.

Enabling Successful Wealth Transfer:

- Align yourself with psychologists and/or psychotherapists who can assist heirs with "Sudden Wealth Syndrome,"[22] which involves the stress, guilt, social isolation and confusion that will often accompany a giant windfall.

- Money conversations are not comfortable but they are vital to ensure that your clients' families will be taken care of financially before the end of their lives. While clients are healthy, encourage them to have crucial conversations with their heirs. They are "crucial" when the stakes are high, strong opposing opinions are present and emotions run strong.[23] It is essential that they take place in a safe environment where everyone is valued and their input is respected. As their wealth manager, you may be able to assist with these conversations or perhaps introduce the family to a professional facilitator.

- Along with these conversations, encourage Boomers to have regular family meetings, starting with couples and then moving on to the entire family. Heirs need to be involved, even at a young age, because eventually they will be substitute decision-makers and possibly executors, both of which carry a great deal of responsibility.

- Because younger heirs will probably push for new investment strategies, in order to connect with them and keep them involved, encourage clients to consider adding something to their portfolios that will philosophically appeal to them, such as socially responsible investments.

- In preparation for being an estate coach, learn the differences between how an advisor and a coach conduct themselves when working with clients. You will need both skill sets at different times in your client relationships.

---

[22] Schorsch, Irvin G., "Too Much, Too Soon: How to Avoid Sudden Wealth Syndrome," HuffPost Money Canada Blog, *The Huffington Post*, July 7, 2012, http://www. huffingtonpost.com/irvin-g-schorsch/sudden-wealth-syndrome_b_1652701.html

[23] Patterson, Kerry, Joseph Grenny, Ron McMillan, & Al Switzler, *Crucial Conversations: Tools for Talking When Stakes Are High*, Second Edition, McGraw Hill, 2012

- Assist your clients to write family wealth mission statements. It is much like writing a person brand statement, but in this case the family members clearly outline their collective values, desires and passions as they relate to wealth and the management of it.[24] These wealth mission statements will be used to guide all family discussions, decisions and actions.

- Become familiar with bereavement etiquette because when Traditionalists and Boomers pass away, it will be necessary for you to politely extend your condolences and even attend funerals. Before talking about financial details involved with the death of a loved one, simply saying, "I'm so sorry for your loss" can genuinely acknowledge the person's grief and bring comfort. If you are unable to contain your emotions and you cry, don't worry. It is better to show that you care than to appear stoic in an attempt to maintain your composure.

As wealth managers, you are experts and skilled professionals facing challenging, yet exciting times. While you ponder client advocacy, financial literacy, creating positive customer experiences, and preparing and supporting families through the transfer of wealth, seek opportunities to continually gain the best industry-related skills because "confident advisors who learn to question their clients more purposefully and listen more actively to deliver the right tax and financial planning solutions,"[25] will be more effective. Whenever you are in the community – at networking events, business meetings, fundraisers, volunteering, and even shopping for groceries – remember that you are always "on" and being watched. If clients and potential customers see that instead of being self-promoting or rude, you show respect and are authentically interested in them, you will stand out. This will give you the presence that you will need to assist them through the greatest wealth transfer period in history.

---

[24] Williams, Roy & Vic Preisser, *Preparing Heirs: Five Steps to a Successful Transition of Family Wealth and Values*, Bandon, OR: Robert D. Reed Publishers, 2003 & 2012.

[25] Jacks, Evelyn, Knowledge Bureau White Paper, Winnipeg, MB, 2013

Chapter 9 – At A Glance

Develop a Framework for Behavioural Finance

The negative emotions attached to money – fear and greed – can derail the ultimate rewards of true wealth: peace of mind. Fear can be offset with the right professional advisory team that provides a strategic plan and process for consistent wealth management, and frequent and reliable communications that enable responsible decision-making.

Urgent Need for Financial Literacy

In the next 35 years, we will see the greatest wealth transfer from one generation to the next. To build on the capital accumulated by the current generation and secure financial futures, there is an urgent need for everyone in the family to be financially literate and familiar with the guidelines associated with joint decisions with tax and financial advisors. True wealth requires a framework for managing the link between financial assets, personal and family health and collective peace of mind.

Empowering Presence Applies to Individuals and Businesses

Investors need to know that their wealth managers have their best interests in mind. Because many people are not satisfied with their financial advisors, these professionals need to empower their own personal brand and image to create trust and establish meaningful relationships so that they will be able to provide exemplary knowledge and service-based solutions that their clients expect and deserve. The principals for empowering presence to find true wealth also apply to businesses; however, in the case of businesses this outcome is rewarded by client loyalty, ensuring a long and happy business life.

Realizing Your True Wealth Potential

We are approaching the end of *EMPOWER YOUR PRESENCE*. However, my hope for you is that this is just the beginning of realizing your true wealth potential and creating more presence in order to impact people in positive ways. Throughout this book, you saw that true wealth extends far beyond money and what you can acquire with it, to developing deep, lasting relationships, being fully involved in life, and having an all-encompassing peace of mind. Some people miss out on this experience; however, you have taken an important first step by reading this book. Commit to putting into practise what you've learned, and you will not be disappointed. In addition to defining true wealth, let's look at what else you have already accomplished.

You Identified People with Presence

You took time to think about people in your life who have presence and identified what it is about their magnetism and charisma that is attractive to you. It might be that they possess a contagious zest for life, like my favourite aunt who used to blow in from faraway places, dressed to the nines, talking excitedly about what she had just seen and what she was about to do next, always laughing and having fun. It could be that in the midst of chaos they have an ability to encourage your faith or envelop you with a deep sense of peace, giving you time to think. Maybe when they listen to you, even in a crowded room, it is as if no one else is present, as I experienced with Princess Anne. Perhaps they are a captivating speaker who seems to make time stand still when they begin to talk. In any case, continue to ask yourself if the qualities that make them memorable are ones that you might wish to emulate and then set a goal to do so, in your own unique way.

You Created Brand YOU!

You identified the strengths, personality traits, and values that are inherently *you* and the passions that motivate your actions. You then went on to develop a personal brand statement to express your unique promise of value – what people will consistently experience when they interact with you. Few people do this. Maybe the daily pressures of life leave them with little time for reflection, so understandably the elements that could empower them lie dormant. You also developed a series of self-introductions to use when meeting people in different environments by distilling the essence of your personal brand into a few words and adding the values and benefits that you bring to others.

You Aligned Your Image and Environment with Your Brand

You learned about the permanence of first impressions and how the ABCs of image - appearance, behaviour and communication – can be used to increase your professionalism and communicate your brand message to people you meet. You saw that fashion and image are quite different, with image centering on thoughtfully defining your personal style. Because your public image is an outward reflection of your authentic inner self, you discovered the importance of ensuring that your image genuinely mirrors what you want others to see and experience when they meet you. You're aware of how to appear powerful and approachable, dress down or up on "the ladder of formality," and fine tune the smallest details of your appearance so that you will always have a look of quality.

You comprehend the difference between etiquette and manners and the role that civility, which involves respect, restraint and responsibility, plays in building trust and maintaining meaningful relationships. The finer points of business protocol, dining etiquette, and how to work a room were covered in detail so that you can always be at ease in social and professional settings, enabling you to forget about yourself and fully concentrate on the people around you.

You recognize how complicated the communication process is so that you can avoid any "noise" that would interfere with the messages you want others to receive. You appreciate that your body language is more powerful than your words in communicating to others what you are thinking and feeling. You know how to use non-verbal communication to make immediate "family" connections with strangers. You received tips on how to have empathetic conversations, make powerful presentations, write clearly and accurately, send professional email, and assess your online image to make sure that it supports your professionalism and personal brand.

You Acquired Cross-generational Intelligence

You caught a glimpse of the characteristics of Traditionalists, Boomers, Generation X, Generation Y and Generation Z, and how their generational makeup influences the way they act in the workplace, as well as specific appearance, behaviour and communication strategies geared to each cohort. This generational intelligence will enable to you to plan, interact and communicate in the most effective ways possible so that the power of all the generations is harnessed so that it can be used to enrich work and relationships.

You are Aware of the Need for Financial Literacy

Depending upon whether you are a client or a wealth advisor, you realize the urgent need to either develop or facilitate financial literacy. Wealth advisors received an overview of what clients expect of financial professionals after the 2008 recession and that research shows that effective communication skills are crucial in increasing client loyalty. You were given practical suggestions on how you can be seen as "the financial literacy expert" so that you can become instrumental in increasing your clients' financial knowledge, something that is sorely lacking and is now deemed to be an essential life skill.

You know that developing long-term relationships with clients lies with them seeing you as their advocate, instead of just being a number in your file. You appreciate the importance of taking a first impression audit of your whole facility, including how your office is set up. You grasped how creating strong customer experiences and hosting client-centred events could help you continually earn their trust so that nothing hinders possible referrals.

Lastly, you were challenged to play a vital role in the successful transfer of your client's wealth from one generation to the next. You comprehend the importance of helping your clients organize regular family meetings where they can begin to have those difficult conversations about money, create family wealth statements to guide them, and prepare their heirs ahead of time for the onerous task of managing their affairs. When the time comes to put things into action, they will be thankful for your involvement and the phenomenal difference it will make to their peace of mind, and of course how it will add to their true wealth.

The Next Steps

Now that you see what you've already accomplished, is there anything else to think about? There is always something more to understand. You recognize that realizing your true wealth potential can mean something totally different to you than for an acquaintance or even your closest friend, because arriving at the place we call "potential" is a very personal and individual process. You know that when you have high self-esteem it will enable you to connect with others because you will feel that you have something of value to contribute. You are also aware that having presence is not an act that you put on when it is convenient, but it is about being authentic. It is linked to a wholeness that comes from aligning your inner thoughts and feelings, and what is important to you at any given moment, with your external brand and image.

What if you are not yet at that place? Presence is not about having everything together. Remember, it is an evolving life-long process. It is about embracing the gifts you possess at this point in time and being fully available to others, expectant that the interaction will encourage them and bring something of value to them. While you wait for those opportunities, review *EMPOWER YOUR PRESENCE* and continue working on bringing everything into align-ment. It takes intention to reach your potential and time to ensure that you are conveying a unified message.

Guiding Principles Going Forward

1. Be Consistent

As you go through life, maintain a clear vision of your personal brand and ensure that your marketing message is clearly and consistently conveyed through your image, always communicating your intrinsic value to others. An "off day" in a public environment can damage your credibility and set you back, especially in new or challenging situations. An image that speaks of quality and authenticity will always have a positive impact on your presence and true wealth.

2. Be Available

Never underestimate the power of being genuine. When you are true to yourself, you'll have peace of mind because you'll have nothing to prove. This will give you the freedom to be fully available to others so that you can encourage, motivate, and empower them to increase their own presence and true wealth. When you show unconditional respect to others and treat them with dignity, it will further increase your circle of influence and presence.

3. Be Persistent

As things change over time, it's important to be persistent in reviewing and testing your values and passions, not as a self-centred narcissistic act, but rather to see whether your personal brand statement and image require updating to be in line with new realities. Empowerment doesn't simply come from applying a few strategies that you glean from a self-help book, but from living intentionally. When things don't go according to your plan, don't be discouraged and give up. Review your goals, abandon things you can't control, and try some new tactics.

The Results of Realizing Your True Wealth Potential

You Will be Credible

When you define your unique talents, showcase them through your personal style and consistently respect others, you will gain credibility. This doesn't mean that you need to be overbearing to be believed. Remember, shy people often become experts in their fields to compensate for what they see as a lack of social skills. When others discover their wealth of knowledge, they're seen as go-to people who always have solutions to complex problems.

You Will Command Attention

Your personal brand – *Brand YOU!* – has the power to command attention. Just as successful commercial brands strive to be irrepressibly attractive to create top-of-mind awareness, when you spend time defining who you are and always use your appearance, behaviour and communication to deliver on your brand promise, you will be remembered. Without being overpowering, you will positively influence people and situations. When you have surety and direction in your life, there will be something magnetic about you– people will want to be with you and learn from you, so that they too can acquire the same attributes.

You Will Be Confident

When you have a strong personal awareness and know how to act with graciousness in any context, you will be completely at ease. This will be expressed through your voice, body language and actions. Egotistical confidence is a device used by those who are insecure and it repels people rather than being engaging. The realistic confidence you will exude is always attractive, generating more relationships, more influence, and throughout your career, more opportunities to earn money.

You Will Empower Others

The connections that result from attracting people to you will give you opportunities to influence them in so many ways. Will you confine them to follow your vision? Or will you encourage them to believe in themselves and discover what makes them unique, so that they too can open new doors, build relationships, and realize their own true wealth potential? Remember, the line between inspiring and manipulating others is fine. Decide to take the more honourable road, moving the focus away from self-seeking opportunism and embrace a spirit that believes we can all benefit from one another. In empowering others, you'll continue to empower yourself and further increase your presence and true wealth.

Every time you cross paths with someone, you have an opportunity to touch them in a memorable way with your presence. It doesn't take money or fame, but rather, a choice. You can either pass the person by, or you can invest valuable time listening, empathizing, and being fully present with them in a rich and meaningful way. This is the essence of having an empowered presence and irrefutably is at the basis of having true wealth.

Chapter 10 – At A Glance

Realizing True Wealth is an Ongoing Process

Identifying people – or enterprises – with presence, creating *Brand YOU*, aligning the ABCs of your image with your brand, acquiring cross-generational intelligence, and empowering your financial behaviour are five key steps in the journey to realize true wealth that is endearing and enduring.

Be Intentionally Consistent, Available and Persistent

It takes intention to reach your potential and time to ensure that your personal brand always conveys a unified message. Going forward, you need to be consistent with your brand message, fully available to others, and persistent in reviewing and testing your values and passions. If they change over time, bring your brand and image into line with your new brand reality.

A Generous Spirit Empowers Others, and It's Reciprocal

When you continue to define your unique characteristics and showcase them through your personal brand and image, you will be credible, confident and command attention. Most importantly, every time you cross paths with someone, you will have an opportunity to be available to help empower them in realizing their true wealth potential. This kind of generosity reciprocates by attracting people – and business – to you.